TRIATHLON RUNNING FOUNDATIONS

A Simple System for Every Triathlete to Finish the Run Feeling Strong, No Matter Their Athletic Background

TAREN GESELL

Published worldwide by Taren Gesell
Print ISBN: 978-1-7770901-1-1
Ebook ISBN: 978-1-7770901-2-8

CONTENTS

CHAPTER 1

INTRODUCTION

"I'm great on the swim and the bike, but I fall apart on the run."

"I need to work on my run, but I always get injured, so I can't."

If these types of comments have bounced off the inside walls of your head, you're not alone. Hopes and dreams of a good finish are often snuffed out within the first few kilometers of the run.

Triathletes face a lot of common struggles. Lack of energy coming off the bike. Cramped up legs. Feeling sluggish. Unable to get up on their toes. Feeling like the 42.2-km/26.2-mile IRONMAN run is basically a death march. If there's one spot in a triathlon when races tend to fall apart—it's most often during the run.

A bad run, whether due to training or race strategy missteps, has huge consequences on a triathlete's success in a race. For most, the difference between a great swim and a terrible swim might be a matter of five to 15 minutes. A killer bike and a bad bike, perhaps 20-40 minutes. A bad run? It could add hours to a triathlete's finish time.

For example, take a triathlete who shuffles through an IRONMAN run at a slow-but-steady seven minute per kilometer pace. Compare that to an athlete who can run just half of the IRONMAN run portion at that seven minute per kilometer pace— but has to walk the other half of the marathon. This triathlete is likely looking at a seven-and-a-half-hour marathon, flirting with not making the cut off.

Compared to swimming and biking, a strong run is the number one determinant of a successful race. The run is a large percentage of an athlete's total race time. It's imperative that athletes who want to do as well as possible in their races (and actually enjoy racing without the dreaded Frankenstein death march at the end), have a successful run.

Maybe you're thinking you're not built for running like feather-light super-runners Patrick Lange, Mark Allen, Gwen Jorgensen, or Miranda Carfrae are. Or you might be saying that every time you try to run more you get injured, so you'll never be able to run *enough* to run well.

And that's fair. Running at a super high level requires a slight body type and resilience to deal with the pounding that occurs when logging high run mileage. But 99% of us aren't trying to run at a super elite level. Most of you reading this are weekend warriors; triathletes who want to feel a bit like a badass by crossing the finish line feeling strong. To do that, you don't need the genetic gifts required of world class athletes. I know this from personal experience.

When I first took up triathlon in 2009, I couldn't run. Really. I. Literally. Could. Not. Run. Standing 5 feet 8, I was tipping the scales at 215 pounds with bad shin splints and lower-back pain. I had to start by running the length of one house, then walking two houses. Slowly, I built myself up to running to the end of the block. Eventually, after a year of training, I did my first *try-a-tri* (400m swim, 13km bike, 3km run) which ended in the hardest 3 km (1.8 mile) cramp-fest of a run I've ever done.

Fast forward to 2011. I completed my first ever half marathon in 1:52:11. That was good for 708th place out of a few thousand. It was decent to finish in under two hours, but I was far from being a *good* runner. I still thought running wasn't for me. Although I had lost some weight by this time, I was still a bulky 180 pounds. I had stubby legs with a 30-inch inseam. I still suffered from shin splints every time I ran longer than eight kilometers. During that half marathon, my lower back seethed with so much pain that I didn't think I'd ever do another long running race again. Over the following winter, however, something happened.

Maybe it was the chill in the air (Winnipeg is FRIGID in the winter), but I decided I would start taking triathlon training seriously. I wanted to push my body and see what I was able to do, take myself to a place I never thought possible. I was compelled to make my workouts longer, faster and more challenging. And certainly more intentional.

The next year (after that 1:52 half marathon) I went back to the same event, on the same course, in hotter conditions, and did something I didn't think I'd ever even come close to. I ran a 1:32:39, placing 93rd overall. That summer, I ran close to 20-minute 5K times in Sprint triathlons, and netted sub 20-minute 5K road running races.

Over the following years, my running got even better. I eventually ran a personal best half marathon time of 1:28:05 (in that same half marathon where I had made my debut a few years earlier), good for 17th overall. I got my 5K road running times close to 19 minutes. I shaved my Olympic triathlon 10K runs down to around 41 minutes. My half marathons in 70.3 events shrunk to under 1:35.

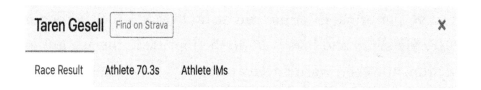

2018 IRONMAN® 70.3 World Championship
Taren Gesell
#1825 - M35-39

	Time	Race Time	Div. Pos	Div. Rank	DPI	
Swim	28:59	28:59	92	92	89.8	+
T1	2:59	31:58	78	40		+
Bike	2:26:58	2:58:56	45	63	96.2	+
T2	2:18	3:01:14	36	10		+
Run	1:34:44	4:35:58	112	229	89.8	+
Overall	4:35:58		112 / 385		94.9	+

My running had come so far. I was quite thrilled with the progress I'd made. But when I started to competing for age group wins to earn berths to world championship events (and even when I finally raced in my first world championship in 2018), my run performances in triathlons didn't shine.

While I was competitive in the swim and bike, my run would let me down when I was up against the best. Take a look at the relative performance of my run at IRONMAN 70.3 Worlds in 2018. My swim and bike were in the top 100 in the age group. My run, however, wasn't even average—it was below average.

After that 2018 70.3 Worlds run, I dedicated myself (once again) to improving it over the winter of 2018-19. After an entire winter of 20-plus kilometer long runs, diligent low-heart-rate training, and hard interval runs, I tried to qualify for 70.3 Worlds again while racing IRONMAN 70.3 Puerto Rico.

My training paid off. I reeled off the best 70.3 swim performance of my life, clocking a 31-minute non-wetsuit swim. After the bike, I found myself in second place overall. Everything fell apart, however, when I got to the run. I mustered a 1:41:27 run split, getting passed for the last two spots to Worlds during the final kilometer of the run.

Once again, I wondered if my body structure, my genetics or my fitness wouldn't allow me to become the competitive runner I wanted to be. I also had a mere three months until my first full IRONMAN distance race at Challenge Roth in Germany (which was going to test my run fitness more than any race I'd ever done). Would I have to go full-throttle on the swim and bike, and then schlep myself through the run?

Fortunately, prior to Challenge Roth, I hooked up with two of the best coaches I've ever met. Dr. Dan Plews took over my overall training. He's a coach to many pro triathletes, a sport scientist in exercise physiology and the current IRONMAN

Kona amateur course record holder. I also brought in Paul Mackinnon (aka The Balanced Runner) to fine tune my run technique.

By the time Challenge Roth rolled around, my run was feeling good. But I had still never run any further than 33 km in one shot, and I was about to compete in my first IRONMAN distance event. To my surprise, (and the surprise of a lot of people around the world), I finished in a time of 9:41 — placing 229 out of 2617.

The breakdown of how the 9:41 performance came to be is incredible. After being the 437th athlete out of the water, I put in a 5:06 bike split which moved me up a few spots. Neither performance stood out as a great breakout effort though. The amazing part was that, after Transition 2, I went on to have the best run of my whole life to that point.

I ran the entire 42.2 kilometers non-stop. That's without cramps, without fatigue and without slowing my pace whatsoever. I ran 5-minute kilometers like clockwork from the very first step until the final painful 1,000 meters. I had the 211th fastest run of the day, passing roughly 150 athletes. That 3:24:31 marathon was in the top-nine percent of runners in the entire Challenge Roth field. For the first time in my life, the run was the standout aspect of my race.

Some people might say I must have lost weight so that's why I had faster run times. In 2011-12, this was true. I went from 175 pounds to 160 pounds, which certainly helped me shave 20 minutes off my half marathon time. But leading into Roth, I had actually put on six or seven pounds—yet still I ran better than I ever have.

Other people might say my run volume must have increased dramatically. Again, in 2011-12, this was true. I made my runs longer and faster. Leading into Challenge Roth, I was running more than ever. But between 2012 and 2019, when I got slightly faster (but didn't make many big leaps in run performance), I tried both running a lot and running very little. In both cases, the strategy resulted in basically the same run times.

What you should take from this story is that running isn't about *being built to run*. It's really not. It's not about being super light or even about having to log huge miles day after day pounding the pavement. Whether you're trying to break two hours for the first time in a half marathon, make that first big leap in run performance, or wanting to compete for age group wins, running is about two things: the right training and the right technique.

As I've proven, triathletes can run miles and miles without getting faster. In fact, with the wrong training or technique, they could actually risk illness and/or injury.

After reading this book, you won't have to deal with those issues. We're going to teach you the right way to train. You're going to build speed, endurance and strength to get across your finish line feeling strong.

You'll learn a run technique that will allow you to feel light and springy so you don't end your long runs feeling like you lost a hammer fight. Your fast runs will feel like you're bounding off the ground faster than ever before.

Finally, you'll learn which running gear will support your training instead of holding it back—and which running gear to avoid (thus saving you some cash).

Before getting into all that though, I want to say that this book isn't solely about teaching you the methods I alone used to learn to run well. This triathlon running system is scientifically studied and proven to work for huge numbers of people (where relevant, I'll share those studies). And, we've also confirmed that these methods work for large numbers of people through our online training app, the MōTTIV training app (app.mymottiv.com) which you can check out for free for 14 days, at any time.

We've met dozens of athletes (and had messages from hundreds more) who've told us they're smashing personal best run records. They're running faster with lower heart rates. They're getting injured less often. They now enjoy running, and they feel confident in their run abilities for the first time ever.

We need to address a fact you may never have considered: *triathlon running isn't really like running.* You might be saying, "What the heck are you talking about, Taren?!"

When you race in a pure 5K, 10K, half-marathon, marathon, or to a lesser extent an ultra-marathon, you're doing a speed-focused run. Those races can last as short as 15 minutes, or as long as four to six hours, with the whole point being to go as fast as possible during the entire event. These runners start their races with fresh, snappy-fast legs. And, even in the longest races, the athletes often don't have to worry about muscular failure because by the time their muscles really start getting tested, the race is over. This is completely different from the triathlon run.

In a triathlon, athletes start the run on already-tired legs, and may also be experiencing muscle damage from a hard bike. Their run pace is at a sub-maximal effort level due to the run commencing immediately after a ton of exercise. Ultimately, the triathlon run is less about racing and more about grinding out a steady pace without slowing down—as opposed to being speedy.

Two-time Olympian Sarah True, and wife of American 5K record holder/ professional runner Ben True, describes triathlon running as a "strength run" which is very different from the "speed run" that Ben performs.

In interviews with us, Sarah and Ben have described how their run training is vastly different. The volume of running required is different. The technique required for triathlon running is different. The race strategy itself is completely different. Preparing for a strength run versus a speed run is almost as different as training for a Sprint triathlon versus an IRONMAN.

Observant readers might point to the run times of super elite triathletes such as International Triathlon Union (ITU) speedster, Alistair Brownlee, who ran a 10K time at the Rio Olympics that was close to the gold medal winning time on the track. This might make you question how different the triathlon run can be. Isn't running fast *just running fast*? Yes and no.

For starters, almost everyone reading this is not a professional ITU triathlete or an elite, long course, professional IRONMAN athlete. Age groupers are running at a slower pace (they're more plodding and steady), with longer ground contact times). That means the skills amateurs need are different than the run abilities required to be world class. We age group triathletes need to stop ourselves from slowing down. We don't need to be terribly concerned with running like a gazelle. If we did try to push those paces, we'd probably blow ourselves up on the race.

Next, most pure running books or articles talk about how elite runners log 100-plus mile weeks on a regular basis, and run at least once (if not twice) a day. The authors might also say the number one determinant of run performance is mileage—and the more mileage (within reason) the better. Ben True, for example, has a schedule which includes 14 runs over the course of a nine-day training cycle. However, there is a big "BUT" in that training cycle we triathletes need to take note of.

In Ben's 14-workout training cycle, only about three of those runs are difficult: one long run, one fast track run and one tempo run. All the rest are just general, low-intensity short runs that elite runners use to keep a high level of overall fitness and low body weight. It's these extra runs that build up the huge mileages logged by elite runners.

Triathletes, on the other hand, build a huge amount of general fitness from training for all three sports at the same time. An elite triathlete looking to step-up their running game could get away with the same approach. One long run, one fast track run and one tempo run each week, then throwing in an extra weekly brick run starting a few months before a big race. The triathlete could completely forget about doing all those extra general fitness and mileage building runs because the swimming and the cycling builds that extra fitness.

That said, if you start reading run-specific training methods and worry you need to drastically increase your miles in order to run better, I'm here to tell you that's not the case. We'll give you a system with a maximum of three workouts per week that'll make you a great triathlon runner.

Running technique for triathletes is also very different than the techniques required to be an elite runner.

Watching a runner such as Ben True is like watching a moving work of art. He's up on his toes, covering huge distances with each stride, breathing lightly. His elastic energy makes him look like a spring that's wound up and released in a coordinated way, every third of a second. Amateur triathletes don't need to run like this (and, frankly, probably can't run like this). Using elite running techniques as a basis for how we need to run isn't realistic.

Elite runners are typically wound tight. Their tendons are taut and have so much elastic energy that a lot of them are quite inflexible. But, damn does that tightness help them spring off the ground. Their calves are also often narrow and light. Most of us aren't built like this. We can't expect to run like the elites.

Now, I'm going to point out something that might cause the barefoot/natural running community to use this book exclusively for fire-starting purposes. For most of us, that forefoot foot strike (where elite runners land and spring off their toes with each stride) might look great, but it isn't as efficient (or as fast) as a mid- or even a heel-strike running stride.

The argument made by the purist barefoot and natural running community is that the forefoot running stride is better for runners because the impact on the ground is softer, while the impact on the ground with a heel strike is very sharp. That's true.

The impact curve from a forefoot running stride is smoother and less instant, while the impact curve with a heel strike is indeed quite sharp. However, studies show the total impact force with both running styles is the same. There's no real change in the load placed on the body with either stride style.

What has also been found is, when studies measured how much energy it took runners to land on their forefoot, mid foot or heel (at paces slower than roughly six minutes per mile), it was more efficient to run with a mid-foot or heel striking method of running.

The more important factor with regard to where runners land with each foot strike is where the foot lands in relation to the body—not where it lands in relation to the foot itself. So, whether you land first on your heel, your mid foot or your forefoot, it doesn't matter as long as your foot lands underneath your body, as opposed to in front of or behind it.

An entire section in this book is dedicated to correct running technique. You can go to mymottiv.com/runfoundations to watch the videos we've created to explain and guide you through developing a run technique that's efficient, reduces injuries, lowers your heart rate and allows you to go faster without as much effort.

By now, you get it: triathlon running is different. Understanding this will allow you to rebuild your foundation of running knowledge and set you up for strong running in your upcoming races.

Some changes you'll experience as a result of this book (for example, minor technique corrections) will generate instant improvements for you. Other changes (such as increasing the proportion of running you do at lower heart rates) will take longer to generate noticeable changes. In some cases, the changes you make as a result of this book might be so subtle that you don't even notice they're happening because the improvements occur bit-by-bit and over time. Know that with the consistent implementation of the system in this book, you will make improvements to your running no matter where your individual start line is.

Let's take those first few steps!

CHAPTER 2

TRIATHLON RUN TRAINING

As we launched the MōTTIV training app and started thinking about how to coach a large quantity of athletes at once, I started feeling pressure to ensure the training programs resulted in the race results each athlete wanted.

I read as many triathlon training books as possible, consuming endless doses of information. But all of the advice seemed too anecdotal. Very few of the books and articles had any scientific backing. Of course, a lot of the resources were written by coaches or writers with a solid background in the sport. But were those coaches right simply because their small group of athletes had been successful with those methods? Or, were they successful despite them?

What's more, I questioned whether these resources were based on elements supporting long term health, performance and enjoyment for amateur triathletes. Or, were they based on what the writers had found resulted in world class performance but weren't realistic for amateur triathletes?

Eventually, I realized I had to do my own research. And it's paid dividends, evidenced by the hundreds of our MōTTIV training app athletes setting personal bests while not feeling tired during training—and with radically lower rates of sickness and injury.

The systems we've created are sprinkled throughout the Triathlon Foundations series of books (*Triathlon Swimming Foundations, Triathlon Bike Foundations and Triathlon Nutrition Foundations*). One of the eye-opening findings I learned was with regards to training generally, but running in particular. Although having successful races is strongly related to an athlete's volume of training (hours per week), what's more important is the *composition* of that training. A well-structured training plan with limited hours is far better than a poorly structured training plan with a lot of hours of weekly training.

A proper structure to run training is critical because running is tremendously hard on the body. It drives our heart rates higher than swimming or biking, and our body structure is required to carry at least three to four times our bodyweight with each stride. Running is harder on your cardiovascular, neuromuscular and musculoskeletal systems. It's brutally hard on the body.

We have to be careful to ensure we don't overload our body, which could result in sickness and injury. We still need to train hard enough to get ready for our races.

How do we accomplish both seemingly difficult tasks?

Three workouts a week unpacked like this: A long run, an intense run and a brick run. If done at the right intensity, distance, with the right rest intervals and on the right running surface and terrain, every triathlete can become a strong and durable runner.

In this chapter, we'll dive into each of these types of runs so you'll know how to get the most out of your time hitting the pavement. You'll understand the requirements to become a strong runner, and how to build those requirements easily—without having to rack up huge miles and while avoiding injury.

REQUIREMENT #1: BUILD ENDURANCE WITH THE LONG RUN

When non-triathletes first hear about our sport, their first reaction is often, "You need to swim, bike, and run for *HOW LONG?!*" A lot of triathletes log more miles in the pool each week than the average person spends walking around. Whether you're just getting into triathlon, or you're already a seasoned triathlete, you're going to have to cover the same distance as every other athlete lining up next to you at the start line. There are no shortcuts in a race—regardless of your fitness or familiarity with triathlons.

The first, and most important requirement, is building up the endurance to complete the run course distance feeling strong. This means making the distance of the run in your chosen race a non-issue.

We want to make you so strong on the run that not only can you run the distance your race requires, but you can feel good running that distance after swimming and biking and having tired legs.

A lot of new triathletes (and even some seasoned ones) think to run well in a triathlon they need to run a lot or run really long. To an extent, this is true. But in this book, we're going to teach you how to manipulate the distance of your long runs, the terrain and surface of your long runs and the pace of your long runs. This will allow you to run well in your races without putting in hundreds and hundreds of hard pounding miles year-round.

Of all the skills you'll need to build in order to have a successful race, establishing the endurance to run long enough to complete your race feeling strong will be the easiest of the methods we're going to teach you.

Finally, if you've purchased this book through Amazon, stop right here. Go to mymottiv.com/runfoundations where you'll find our free Triathlon Training Plan Calculator. Use this guide to help lay out how long you should run (depending on your race distance and the date of that race), and where runs should fit in your weekly training schedule.

REQUIREMENT #2: RUN OFF THE BIKE WITH THE BRICK RUN

Being able to run 5, 10, 21.1 or 42.2 km is very achievable. In fact, I would say it's downright easy with the right sequential build-up from one workout to the next. But doing so after a rough swim and a long bike is much tougher.

Spending a couple hours (or more) in the water and then on the bike, your body gets used to not having to hold up your bodyweight. Then BOOM, you hop off the bike and start running on jelly legs. Your heart rate spikes because your blood flow has to reroute itself in a real hurry and cramps often start to set in.

The ability to run in a triathlon is a completely different skill than running alone. Athletes need to know how to physically run off the bike, and they need to know how to pace themselves properly in the first few kilometers of the run to make sure they don't ruin the rest of their race.

In this book, we'll teach you how to properly incorporate bike-to-run brick workouts in order to teach your body how to function correctly the second you step off your bike in Transition 2, and how to approach those crucial first few steps of the run.

REQUIREMENT #3: BUILD SPEED WITH THE INTENSE RUN

While we all have to complete the same distance in a race regardless of our fitness level, the separating factor between the pros and the amateurs is simply speed. I guarantee, I can get you to run 42.2 km after a 180 km bike, but doing so in sub-four-minute kilometers like two-time IRONMAN World Champion Patrick Lange is going to be much tougher. That doesn't mean we can't make you faster though. Building speed is just a little tougher than building endurance.

When most triathletes first get into the sport (or even jump up from one distance to the next) their goal is to just find a way to make it to the finish line. Once that first race is finished, they typically want to go faster, set personal bests and see what they're capable of. This requires going into the pain cave a bit, pushing our running legs beyond what's comfortable.

Those uncomfortably hard runs are tough because they push us into an effort level that's a tad beyond our current capability. This causes our body to think "Oh wow, if this yahoo is going to make me do stuff like that again, I better get stronger and faster."

This improvement is called a hormetic response. We need to stimulate that hormetic response to get faster.

There's good news here: creating this adaptation to make you faster is easy, because we know exactly how to create it. Just go appropriately hard every so often. The bad news is that sometimes what it takes to create that response can be a challenge, and by challenge, I mean super painful and leave you wanting to toss your cookies on the side of the track. But hey, we're triathletes. If it wasn't hard it wouldn't interest us, right?

In the Intense Run section, we'll talk about what "appropriately hard" means for the intense run. How frequently to run hard, how to make sure the hard runs don't create injuries, rest intervals, and how the intense run evolves over the course of a season.

That's it. Throughout the course of this book you're going to learn how to use these three key workouts to make yourself faster in the triathlon run. Of course, some of you might not have time every week (or any week) to run three times. That's totally OK. We'll help prioritize which workouts can be easily shortened throughout the year without any consequence to your race, and the ones that can be optional without affecting your race.

Despite what proponents of High Intensity Interval Training (HIIT) say, I believe the long run is by far the most critical run that's non-negotiable in a triathlete's training week.

While intense interval run sessions can both make you faster and improve your endurance, there's no substitute for training your body to go through the pounding of a race-distance run. HIIT runs can make you faster and improve your endurance, but they're shorter. They don't place the same load on the musculoskeletal structure that a long run does through the much higher number of impacts on the ground. A long run prepares the musculoskeletal structure to endure the pounding you'll take during a race, and you can add intervals into a long run to get a lot of the same speed benefits you'd get in a HIIT-only session (the same can't be said in reverse for HIIT runs).

If you're prioritizing workouts, and can only do one run workout each week, make it the long run—and do it year-round. While just the term "long run" might have you thinking I'm going to recommend tons of miles week after week, taking time away from your family, work, and your social life, you won't have to run too terribly long very often throughout the season to get your body ready for your race(s).

Believe it or not, endurance will progress easily for almost every one of you out there. While speed and strength are harder to build, raw endurance is simple to build and, as long as you're consistent, requires far less time than you think.

In 2014, I completed a 27-km swim and then, in 2017, a 37-km non-stop open-water marathon swim. You might think I needed to log dozens of swims that were 10, 15, or 20-plus kilometers in the year leading up to each of them. In reality, all I needed to do was swim four times a week for 45-90 minutes. Then, starting three months out, gradually build-up just one swim each week by 10% until I had completed just a total of three swims longer than three hours.

That's literally all it took. Our bodies are meant to be active for hours, even days on end. Our ancestors couldn't stop if they got tired. They could only stop once they had food. Tracking down dinner sometimes took days. My body, your body, every triathlete's body is wired to build up endurance and complete our races easily regardless of the distance.

MAKE YOUR EASY RUNS FASTER

A friend of mine named "Super Dave" Lipchen, Head Coach of the Windburn Multi-Sport Academy (and a great triathlete in his own right), was once coached for a couple of years by a high-performance national level coach. Dave's heart rate is naturally quite a bit higher than the average person's. This resulted in his typical runs being done at heart rates in the 160s, 170s, or even 180s which is tremendously hard to keep up, no matter how fit he got.

The coach's suggestion was this: every single run had to have a heart rate cap of 145 beats per minute. For the first few weeks, Dave was forced to run/walk to keep his heart rate that low. But eventually Dave's body adapted and he was able to bring his jogging heart rate down to 145. Later that year, Dave did an Olympic distance race after using this new training method. His 10K time dropped by a minute, running 41 minutes for the 10K, but it felt so much easier than his previous 42-minute 10K runs.

The next year, Dave continued with the low heart rate runs and saw even more benefit, putting out a 37-minute 10K run in an Olympic distance triathlon which he says felt easier than any other 10K run he had done in his life. In addition to that improved run time, he also put out swimming and biking personal bests. Because the running was done at a lower heart rate, it wasn't beating him up as badly and he was able to work harder on his bike and swim training. That year, he put out a personal best Olympic distance time of 2:04 and says it's the best he's ever run.

This isn't a one-off story, either. Dan Plews, PhD, is a sports physiologist and coach to pro triathletes. He's also the 2018 overall IRONMAN Kona Amateur Champion and course record holder. Dan coached me up to Challenge Roth in 2019. When he started working with pros, he looked at their training times and thought, "No, that can't be all they do. Those paces are slow and I could do them." But he quickly learned that the difference between him doing a training run at, say, a 4:30 km and a pro doing a 4:30 km, is that the pro is working easier than Dan was.

Dan said that pros train a lot, but the vast majority of that training is done at a low intensity and a low heart rate.

Triathlons aren't like the 100-meter dash or even long-distance track running (which are done at a near-maximal effort). Instead, even the shortest Sprint triathlons are a very sub-maximal, controlled-pace effort. The key to racing faster is to make your easy efforts faster, so your fast efforts are easier. You'll end up staying away from your top end maximum heart rates and have a nice, fast pace that you're able to hold for hours on end.

This is the training we do on our online triathlon training website called the MōTTIV training app (app.mymottiv.com) and it works wonders. Athletes all over the world are reporting that they're running faster, at lower heart rates, and without injuries.

One TeamTrainaic.com athlete reported basically the exact same story as my friend Dave's. She said she started training with lower heart rates and, in some cases, it resulted in her walking for parts of the run so she doubted how it would ever make her faster. A couple months later, however, she was completing her runs at paces faster than she expected. She was surprised at how relatively easy they felt. In her first race, she set a 10-minute personal best in the 10K of her Olympic distance triathlon. Later that year, she went on to PB in a 70.3 race by 55 minutes.

PACING THE LONG RUN WITH HEART RATE

This easy running pace is the key to doing successful long runs. Speed and ease will come as a result of it. The first step we need to take right now is to figure out what heart rate cap you're going to use when training by heart rate during the long run.

The ideal way to get your heart rate cap is in a lab that tests your aerobic threshold. Simply put, aerobic threshold is the heart rate at which your effort level goes from a very controlled, aerobic pace that you can maintain all day into a harder pace that isn't sustainable for hours on end. This aerobic threshold heart rate is the easy running pace cap that we want to use for a lot of your long runs.

Unfortunately, lab testing is expensive and not easily available or practical for many athletes. Not to worry. We'll use a calculation to get you close to your exact aerobic threshold pace in about a minute and with zero cost.

I like to use the Maffetone Method heart rate calculation developed by Dr. Phil Maffetone. It's a great way to identify the starting point for your heart rate training cap. It's similar to many age-based heart rate calculations, but with some further customizations to dial in your unique heart rate cap.

Here's how to do the Maffetone Method heart rate calculation:

Step 1: Subtract your age from 180 (E.G. For a 36-year old, do 180 - 36 = 144)

Step 2: If you're recovering from a major illness or injury that's occurred within the past year, subtract 10 from Step 1.

Step 3: If you've modified your training for more than two weeks due to a cold or injury, subtract an additional 5.

Step 4: If you've been training for two years or more without any health problems as in step 2 or 3, add 5.

RESULT: This is what's known as your MAF heart rate.

The MAF heart rate is great, but it is not always perfect and can be a bit off for some people. Personally, there was a time my MAF heart rate was calculated at 145 beats per minute. But under lab testing, my aerobic threshold was 137 beats per minute. Here's how you can deal with that issue.

The final step to dial in your heart rate ceiling is very subjective, but the results will generate a powerful tool come race day. Take your MAF heart rate and start running as if it's 100% accurate. Then pay attention to how your breathing feels. If your breathing is a touch too strong to carry on a conversation, then you'll have to lower your heart rate ceiling. If your breathing is totally comfortable, stick with the MAF number as your heart rate ceiling.

Here's a HUGE caveat to this step: err on the side of caution... extreme caution. And don't aim too high. Let's say you calculate your MAF heart rate to be 140 beats per minute, but 140 feels somewhat easy. If, in actuality, 138 was your actual aerobic threshold, those two beats per minute would be enough to make all of your low heart rate training much less effective; you'll be burning less fat, building less efficient muscle fibre and you'll risk overtraining yourself. So, I'd rather you lower your heart rate ceiling by too much than leave it too high.

Burn this heart rate ceiling into your brain. It's going to be the heart rate you'll set as a cap for how fast you'll run on your weekly long runs. When you start using this heart rate cap as a guide to set your pace, there'll almost certainly be some questions popping up:

Q: When I run on hills, into the wind or on uneven surfaces, I almost have to walk to keep my heart rate under the heart rate cap.

A: The heart rate cap is the heart rate cap regardless of terrain, elevation or other conditions. Give it time and stick with it—even if you have to walk sometimes. Soon, you'll be able to run easily, keeping your heart rate under the cap.

Q: My heart rate gradually climbs as the run goes on and I have a hard time keeping it under the heart rate cap.

A: It's totally normal for heart rate to climb gradually over the first 90 minutes of a workout then level out. This is called cardiac drift. When you first start running with the heart rate cap, this effect will be significant. As you run with the heart rate cap more often, its effect will be less severe. Some runs will maintain the heart rate cap even as it gets harder to do so later in the run. Other runs, called progression runs, will ignore the heart rate cap towards the end of the run, so cardiac drift is less of an issue.

Q: I've been running with the heart rate cap for a couple months and I'm not able to run faster at the same heart rate yet. When will I see progress?

A: Progress doesn't always come in the form of going faster underneath the heart rate cap. It might come by way of being able to run faster when intense running is called for. Perceived effort could be lower at the same heart rates and paces. Or, your progress in swimming or biking could be improving as a result of the work being done on the run. Lowering your paces at the same heart rate is a slow process. Trust that progress IS being made. Typically, you should see some very small gains within the first three to six months. You should really see things progressing at six to 12 months. After a year, you should notice your gains transferring across all sports.

Q: Which heart rate monitor do you recommend?

A: Check out the DC Rainmaker website. He keeps an up-to-date list of recommended devices at all price points. His reviews are spot on.

Q: Why not do all training at low heart rates if it's so effective?

A: Low heart rate training isn't the be-all and end-all. In a study [1] conducted on 61 IRONMAN Copenhagen athletes, researchers found two key elements were strongly related to success in the race: ability to burn a lot of fat (which can be accomplished through low heart rate training) and a high VO2 Max (which is accomplished with high intensity training of 15-second to eight-minute intervals). Athletes need to train both easy and hard. We'll talk more about the breakdown of each later.

Q: I'm reading this mid-race season and you've convinced me, Taren! I want to start working heavily on my low heart rate training right now. Should I go all in and do nothing but low heart rate training to work on it quicker?

A: There's a time and a place for doing almost all of your training at low heart rates. That time is during the off-season and the base building season—not during race season. During race season, we need to have our race pace sharp. Less time is spent training at a low heart rate during the race season.

---

[1] https://www.ncbi.nlm.nih.gov/pubmed/29050040

DISTANCE

The distance of the long run might be one of the most intimidating things new triathletes have to wrap their minds around. A lot of athletes believe they need to run long pounding miles, week in and week out. Fortunately, that's not the case. There'll be some runs throughout the year that are definitely long and challenging, but you don't have to waste countless hours every single week.

As a baseline, you want to run a minimum of a certain distance year-round for the long run. This distance will vary, depending on the longest race you're doing in a year. Here are the guidelines you'll want to run as a baseline minimum for a range of distances. Again, this depends on what the longest distance race is that you're doing in a year:

> - **Sprint**: 3-5 km (1.8-3 miles)
> - **Olympic**: 6-8 km (3.6-4.9 miles)
> - **Half-IRONMAN** (70.3): 12-15 km (7.4-9.2 miles)
> - **IRONMAN**: 14-18 km (8.6-11 miles)

If these distances sound like too much for you, no problem. Start running a distance once per week that's a little bit of a stretch, but not so hard that you feel completely beat up for several days afterward. It's OK to be a little sore the day of the long run or the day after the long run. If you're sore for multiple days after the long run, it's a sign you're overdoing it and hampering your weekly training too much.

Once you've nailed down how much your "tough but fair" long run distance is, simply increase the distance by 10% for two weeks then take a rest week and run only 60% of the previous week. For example, if you're training for a half-IRONMAN (70.3) and can only run 5 km currently, do as follows:

- **Week 1**: 5 km
- **Week 2**: 5.5 km (10% more than the previous week)
- **Week 3 REST**: 3.3 km (60% of the previous week)
- **Week 4**: 6.1 km (10% more than the previous longest long run)
- **Week 5**: 6.7 km (10% more than the previous longest run)
- **Week 6 REST**: 4 km (60% of the previous week)

Repeat this pattern until you've built up your long run to as much as the baseline run distance above. Once you've reached the baseline run distance, you'll want to vary your distance slightly each week to keep the stimulus fresh and the body guessing. This is how we get stronger.

So, for example, if you're racing that half-IRONMAN distance and you've reached the baseline range of being able to run 12-15 km (7.4-9.2 miles), vary the distances you run each week. There's no exact guideline for how much to vary, something random like this will work:

- **Week 1**: 13.5 km
- **Week 2**: 15 km
- **Week 3 REST**: 9 km (60% of the previous week)
- **Week 4**: 14 km
- **Week 5**: 14.5 km
- **Week 6 REST**: 8.8 km (60% of the previous week)

Now for the true endurance-building part of the long run: the over-distance run. In order to complete the run portion of your race, not only do you need to be able to run that distance, you need to be able to run longer than that distance. You'll be running on tired legs after a swim and a bike. The best way to do this is by building up to run even longer than you need to in your race.

As your race gets closer, you'll want to build up the distance of your long run by 10% for two weeks then rest during the third week—the same way you might have to build up to the baseline run. You'll want to do this until you've reached the following recommended over-distance run guidelines for each race distance:

- ➢ **Sprint**: 7-9 km (4.2-5.5 miles)
- ➢ **Olympic**: 14-16 km (8.5-9.7 miles)
- ➢ **Half-IRONMAN (70.3)**: 22-24 km (13.7-14.7 miles)
- ➢ **IRONMAN**: 100% of the expected time you'll take during your race, split over two runs (more on this in a bit).

If you're a Sprint or Olympic distance athlete, you'll want to run this over-distance long run at least four to six times before your race. Half-IRONMAN athletes should do this over-distance long run three to four times. IRONMAN athletes should complete this over-distance long run twice.

Once you've done this build-up of running at a low intensity, keeping long runs throughout the year within the baseline long run guidelines, and with several *over-distance* long runs prior to your race, you'll have amassed a large amount of endurance. Your run portion of your race should be easily achievable.

We've simplified all of this on our run foundations website here: mymottiv.com/runfoundations. There, you'll find a spreadsheet you can fill out and print, outlining how far to run each week.

IRONMAN SPLIT RUNS

I believe there are two preparation approaches for the IRONMAN run. One of them is great for high performance athletes, and the other is perfect for the majority of age groupers.

The first way is by running a lot. This is how I prepared for Challenge Roth. While we only built my long run up to three hours, I was also running 45-90 minutes five other times throughout the week. I literally ran every single day besides one (and the coach I was working with even had an optional run scheduled on that day… which I never did).

This approach works well to build up the legs required to get elite-level performance in an IRONMAN. Running on tired legs was like a religion for me at that point. I constantly felt beat up. But in the end, I had the best run of my life in a race, going 3:24 for the marathon in the full IRONMAN distance at Challenge Roth.

However, this approach isn't practical for most age group triathletes. It takes up so much time and puts the athlete at risk of injury. While it worked well for me, keep in mind that my life and schedule revolve around triathlon. I have flexibility, the support of my wife and paramedical practitioners like massage therapists and physiotherapists, all easily accessible. Still, even with all that, I had a hard time fitting in all the runs, and felt hints of injury during the race. So, I don't recommend this method for most triathletes.

Instead, our plan on the MōTTIV training app gets triathletes 100% ready for the run, while making the time commitment very manageable and lowering injury risks. This method is something I call IRONMAN Split Runs, where you split your long run up over two runs on the same day, capping the duration of the run to two-and-a-half hours. This sounds complicated, but it's easy once you see an example.

Let's say you're targeting a 5:30 IRONMAN run (marathon) time, so 100% of your run duration is 5:30 hours. In this case, follow this build up:

Build up your long run 10% each week as outlined previously.

Once your long runs start going past 2.5 hours in duration, break them into two runs that you perform on the same day.

For example, if you reach a point where your long run is taking three hours, break that run into a 2.5 hour run and a 30-minute run later that day.

This rule stays the same even as your runs grow very long. Let's say you progress to the very peak of the long run training and have grown to 100% of your target race time, being 5.5 hours in this example.

In this case, stick to the rule and perform two runs of 2.5 hours. I realize that this doesn't reach the 5.5-hour target, but we want to prevent you from having to run past 2.5 hours, because past that 2-2.5-hour mark, form and technique start to break down, leading to a high likelihood of injury.

This is going to result in some run-focused days, but doing even just a handful of these long weekend runs will save age group triathletes from having to run nearly every single day, making this approach much more practical. This will also allow your body to recover from the runs during the week, and keep you from having to run with bad form, thus reducing the chance of injury.

Split runs are probably the most complicated thing to try to explain in written form. Fortunately, this entire process is taken care of for athletes on the MōTTIV training app.

SURFACE and ELEVATION

I'll get on my soapbox and talk more about running shoe selection later in the book. A related topic to shoe selection is running surface and terrain selection.

The surge in minimal running shoes that started in 2010, coupled with an increased respect for strength training in endurance sports, are both related to the same thing: people in western society who spend most of their days sitting don't have the physical strength to endure high volumes of training without getting injured.

The stabilizer muscles in our feet aren't forced to be strong because we spend our days in shoes. Our side glutes have turned off because of tight hips from sitting most of the day. And, when we do train, it tends to be in a straight linear forward and back direction.

While there is some merit to minimal shoes, strength training and being on a first name basis with a good sport-specific physiotherapist, you can strengthen your lower body, stabilizer muscles and your entire core just by doing what you're already doing: running. The key is to select a running surface and elevation that promotes strength building while you're running.

Switching up the ground surface you run on (like not always running strictly on roads and sidewalks), also has the added benefit of taking a load off the body. In order of hardest on the body to easiest on the body, these are the running surfaces we'll discuss: sidewalk, road, asphalt, packed gravel or limestone, dirt trails and treadmill.

During the off- and base building seasons, and for about half the strength and speed building season, I recommend you run on as many soft surfaces as possible. Packed limestone and dirt trails are perfect because they provide the best balance between a soft surface that's easy on the body, and stable footing that allows for quick foot turnover. While treadmills (besides slatted treadmills such as the Woodway) are soft and a good option for some running, they change your running stride due to the belt doing some of the work for you. They shouldn't be used for all runs.

As the race season approaches, you'll want to run more often on road surfaces, particularly because running exclusively on soft surfaces won't build up the muscle durability you'll need during your race.

Leading up to IM 70.3 Puerto Rico in 2019, I ran exclusively indoors on a treadmill. I live in Winnipeg, Canada and didn't want to risk certain death by running 20 km outside with the temperature at minus 31 degrees Fahrenheit during my heaviest training in January and February. When I got to the race, my muscles felt extremely beat up, like they couldn't function well. By the time I got back from the race and returned to training, the weather at home was nice enough to run outside so I did a long run on pavement. Instantly, I noticed my body didn't have the built-up muscle strength to endure pavement.

Running on soft surfaces also makes it harder for your foot to snap off the ground quickly. A short ground contact time helps you run fast and reduces the likelihood of injury. Gwen Jorgensen is the Olympic gold medalist in the 2016 Rio Olympics, and one of the best runners triathlon has ever seen. I chatted with her husband about a recent race where Gwen wasn't happy with her performance. He said Gwen spent too much time training in Mammoth Lakes (where all the road surfaces were trails) which made her slower on the ground.

Whereas the off-season, base building season and half of the strength and speed building season is ideally an 80% soft surface to 20% road surface ratio, the second half of the strength and speed building season, and race season could be more like 30% soft surfaces to 70% road surfaces.

Running your long run on hills is another way to build up running strength that will allow you to stay strong to the end of the run. Lifting weights builds strength, but it's only loosely related to swimming, biking and running. Running on hills, however, builds sport-specific strength. Your muscles will be more durable, so they won't get as sore during the race, decreasing the likelihood of physical breakdown. Your body structure will also be stronger. You'll be more upright, running with good form deeper into the race.

Running hills is a similar approach to running on soft surfaces. During the off-season it's not critical to build strength. You can run on whatever elevation you want: step hills, rolling hills, flat elevation, whatever you choose is fine as long as you keep your heart rate low even during the hill climbs.

During the base building, and the strength and speed building season, incorporate hills as much as possible during your long run. These hills don't have to be terribly steep climbs, but there's no reason they can't be. Rolling hills, steep hills, sideways cambered hills, mountain bike trails, they're all great ways to force your body to stabilize itself while on an angle, strengthening your stabilizer muscles and the structure of your lower body.

During this phase, don't worry about pace times or foot speed. Hill running, even at a low heart rate, is tremendously beneficial. At the start of the 2018 race season, I had an Achilles tendon injury that prevented me from running much. I decided to run exclusively on soft surface hills. When my first race, IM 70.3 Coeur D'Alene came around, my longest runs had been 14 and 17 km, respectively, but I was still able to put out an all-time half-IRONMAN personal best run of 1:33:53 which, at the time, was a 2.5-minute personal best.

During race season, you'll want to limit your hill running, and, ideally, perform your long runs on an elevation similar to what your race will be. If your race is hilly, stick with hills. If your race is flat, focus less on hills. You can still incorporate around 30% of your running on hills to keep that muscle strength up.

And that, my friend, is the long run. I know it's a lot to take in. But it's simpler than it seems. There are two things that will help bring this all together for you in about 30 seconds.

First, at mymottiv.com/runfoundations, the calculator will allow you to enter your race distance and date, and it'll calculate a guide for how long your long runs should be each week.

Next, a list of pacing, distance, running surface and elevation guidelines that summarizes everything we've discussed is also available on that website.

So you don't have to write all this down and it's easy to remember, at mymottiv.com/runfoundations we've created a PDF and a smartphone-screen sized image that you can print out or save and put wherever is easy to see.

Now that you're able to run long enough to cover the distance of your race, and more importantly do so easily and so you feel strong right to the finish, let's make sure you can nail that run after a hard bike. We'll get you ready to do that with the Brick Run.

LONG RUN

Season	Intensity	Terrain	Elevation	Distance
Off-season (for 6 weeks after the last race of the year)	All easy running at low heart rates	Your choice of: road, offroad	Ideally flat terrain to give your body a rest, but hills are OK	Sprint: 2-3km Olympic: 6-8km 70.3: 10-12km IRONMAN: 12-15km
Base Building (half the time between end of the off-season and beginning of race season)	All easy running at low heart rates	Soft surfaces, ideally	Rolling hills	Sprint: 3-5km Olympic: 8-10km 70.3: 13-16km IRONMAN: 15-18km
Strength and Speed (Half the time between end of the off-season and beginning of race season)	All easy running at low heart rates	First half: 80% soft surfaces, 20% road. Second half: 50% soft surfaces, 50% road surfaces	Rolling hills	Sprint: 5-8km Olympic: 12-16km 70.3: 17-24km IRONMAN: 18-20km
Race Season (starts 6 weeks before first race of the year)	Mostly easy running at low heart rates. Can incorporate 20-30% at 10 sec/km slower to 20 sec/km faster than race pace.	70% road surfaces, 30% soft surfaces	As similar as possible to your goal race elevation. If your race elevation is flat, still include 30% on hills	Sprint: 5-9km Olympic: 12-16km 70.3: 17-24km IRONMAN: 1:14-3.5hrs

THE BRICK RUN

The first triathlon I did was a Try-A-Tri that was a 300 meter swim, 13 km bike and a 3 km run. I decided in the winter to do the race and spent more than six months swimming, biking and running. I didn't have a background in any of the sports, so I figured I needed to build up each discipline to the point I could easily complete the distance of each leg of the race.

Over those six months, I built myself up to be able to swim for 1,000 meters, bike for 50 minutes and some 5 km runs. On race day, the swim went well. I didn't take any breaks, and I was one of the first five athletes to come out of the water. The bike went even better. I was cramp free, and I moved up into second place. But when I hopped off the bike to get myself into transition, I almost fell over. Three steps off the bike and my legs were completely locked up. I ran the three kilometers with my legs completely straight because my quads cramped so badly that I couldn't bend my legs to run.

The reason for this cramp-fest: my training. Sure, I swam a lot, biked a lot, and ran a lot, but I failed to take into account I'd have to do those things back-to-back. I didn't do a single brick workout in training where I went immediately from the bike to the run. I didn't even know a brick workout was a thing.

Brick workouts are crucial. They get your body efficient at quickly re-routing blood flow, an important function when going from the bike to the run. When swimming, our bodies are horizontal. Ninety-two percent of our bodyweight is displaced from the buoyancy of the water, and our arms are doing most of the work. That keeps the blood in our upper body. During the bike, the blood is in your legs, but your body is scrunched up, and your weight is held up by the bike. When you hop off and start running, it's the first time in potentially hours that your body is completely upright, thus requiring you to hold up the entire weight of your body. This transition happens in an instant. If your body doesn't know how to adjust quickly, cue the cramp fest.

It doesn't matter if you're a good runner, either. I remember chatting with a couple of guys before their first triathlon. One of the dudes was a really good half-marathon runner. The other guy was saying, "I can't wait until you get to the run and start picking off everybody one by one. You're going to destroy this race." He hadn't done any brick workouts, and it showed; he ended up in the middle of the field, his run aggressively average. He didn't pass a single person. Suffice it to say, those two guys were a tad more humble after the race.

Training your body to run well after biking hard is the key to a successful triathlon. You can swim fast and bike hard all you want. If you're not prepared to run well off the bike, you can lose tons of time. All the work you put into your training can be undone by leg cramps, stiff muscles, stomach pain and a heart rate so high that it feels like you're going to explode.

Fortunately, training your body to run well after a hard bike is easy. With just a handful of brick workouts, you'll avoid a lot of the issues I, along with almost every new triathlete, experienced.

EXECUTING BRICK WORKOUTS

The section on the long run was a bit of a haul. This one, though, is fairly short because executing a brick workout properly is easy; you go from your bike workout to your run workout in as little time possible. Simple as that.

At a minimum, if you're brand new to triathlon and have your first race coming up soon, getting in six bike/run brick workouts is likely enough to avoid the majority of the catastrophes that will occur without doing any brick runs. Your body might not feel great when you start running after the bike, but it likely won't be a disaster. That said, this guideline of six brick workouts is a minimum for athletes racing Sprint and Olympic distance triathlons; as you progress up to 70.3 and IRONMAN races, this minimum requirement grows to 20 and 40 brick runs, respectively.

Before getting into more of the details about how to get the most out of your brick workouts, you might ask if you need to also do swim/bike brick workouts. Some coaches will have their athletes bring a bike and a trainer to the pool and have athletes biking on the pool deck in their Speedos and one-pieces. I am not one of those coaches.

Triathletes don't go from swimming immediately into biking. They go from swimming to running out of the water, walking through transition, then into biking. Instead of doing swim/bike brick workouts on the MōTTIV training app, I prescribe deck-ups in swim workouts where athletes will complete an interval, then pull themselves up onto the pool deck and run or jog in place for 10 seconds. For example, one of our sets will be something like 700 meters or yards where, at the conclusion of each 100, perform a deck-up and run or jog in place then immediately jump or dive back into the pool and continue until the 700 is complete.

Deck-ups are essentially a mini swim/run brick workout that'll prepare you to finish the swim with a nice, controlled heart rate for Transition 1. Stay calm in transition then ease into the bike, building up your effort over the first 10 minutes of the bike. You'll be completely fine without having to bounce around on a bike in your Speedo on the pool deck.

Now, let's get into how you'll do your bike/run brick workouts.

ONE BRICK WORKOUT A WEEK ... SOMETIMES

How often should you do brick workouts each week and throughout the season? My answer: as often as possible, but no more than necessary. You're probably rightly responding with, "Can you be a little more vague, Taren?"

As I mentioned earlier, the following range is the minimum number of brick workouts I'd recommend completing before each of the various distance triathlons:

> **Sprint**: 6-9
> **Olympic**: 6-12
> **Half-IRONMAN (70.3)**: 15-20
> **IRONMAN**: 30-40

Getting in these mandatory brick runs is critical in the months leading up to your race. It won't help you much if you knock off six brick runs in December and January, don't do any for three months, then race a Sprint triathlon in May. Your body will retain some of the abilities developed from those six brick runs, but most of the benefits you received from the runs will be gone. You'll want to focus more on brick runs immediately prior to your race.

However, on the MōTTIV training app, once athletes commit to doing more than just one run a week, we always make their second run a brick run… year-round. There are several reasons for this:

The more your body is able to run after a bike ride, the better, so the more you do brick runs, the better.

You can "double-dip" and make a brick workout also function as an intense speed-focused workout, but you can't take a standalone speed focused run and make it a brick workout.

Brick workouts are very time efficient because you're already in workout clothes, and as long as your shoes are nearby, you have all the gear to do a run.

Brick workouts are a better return on time spent than some standalone workouts. For example, an easy paced standalone 10-minute run doesn't have a huge amount of benefit, but an easy paced 10-minute brick workout has quite a bit of benefit.

What we prescribe on app.mymottiv.com (depending on how many times a week the athlete wants to run) is one mandatory long run each week year-round at the distances, intensities and terrain indicated in the last section. The second prescribed run in a training week is a brick run—which is optional during the off-season to give the body a break from the pounding of high amounts of running. The third run in a week is a standalone speed-focused intense run. And if the athlete wants to run four times a week the final run is another brick workout, which I'll explain.

TWO BRICK WORKOUTS A WEEK?!

If one brick workout a week is good, then two must be better right? Yes, but it's unnecessary.

Triathletes who train with us on the MōTTIV training app will notice if they choose to run four times a week that there are two brick workouts included in their weekly schedule. I like prescribing our athletes a second brick workout—not because getting in a second brick workout each week is that important— but because most triathletes are tight on time and logistically it's easier to get in an extra run each week just by tacking on a brick run to a bike workout. This extra run workout can also be shorter than a standalone run while still offering a lot of benefit.

The sole reason I include two brick runs a week for triathletes who want to run four times a week is because it's time efficient.

BRICK WORKOUT DISTANCES

While training for the IRONMAN distance race at Challenge Roth in 2019, my shortest standalone run was 45 minutes. The average standalone run, though, was more like 90 minutes. Whereas the longest brick run I did was just eight kilometers, taking me 45 minutes to complete. By including more runs as brick runs, you reduce the amount of time you need to spend training. You can also reduce the distance you need to run (less pounding on the body) and thus a lower chance of injury while still building up your running ability.

Use the following guidelines for how long to make your brick workouts throughout the year with the shorter distance being good in the base building season, progressing up to the longer distance in the race season (remembering that brick runs are totally optional in the off-season):

- ➤ **Sprint**: 1-3 km (0.6-1.8 miles)
- ➤ **Olympic**: 1-4 km (0.6-2.5 miles)
- ➤ **Half-IRONMAN (70.3)**: 2-7 km (1.2-4.3 miles)
- ➤ **IRONMAN**: 3-8 km (1.8-4.9 miles)

Some people believe in running super long during brick runs. I am not one of those people. I occasionally see people on Instagram who are training for a half-IRONMAN, performing a 100-plus km bike ride followed by a one hour run; basically, an actual half-IRONMAN. Or, doing the opposite, performing a 60- to 90-minute bike to "prepare the legs" before a full long run.

Personally, I feel this is overkill. A detriment to progress. Workouts need to have a specific purpose that can be executed well: long runs need to be, well, quite long and performed with good form. Intense runs need to be, you guessed it, intense, with good form. These super long brick workouts are overkill because your form will most likely deteriorate, potentially leading to injury and developing bad movement patterns.

I had four successful years of making progress in triathlon. And then came 2017. My training went off the rails. The program I was on had me performing one-hour rides before my long runs, and one-hour runs after almost every bike I did. When I look back at running footage of me before 2017, my form was powerful with nice tempo. But since that time, my form has been stiff and forced. I think that year of constantly running tired engrained bad muscle movement patterns that I'm still trying to fix.

Rather than perform epic, long brick runs, I'd rather you perform shorter brick runs to make sure they're executed with good form, snappy fast feet, an upright posture and powerful arm movements.

Long runs build endurance. Intense runs build speed. Brick runs teach you how to run after a bike. You don't need a super long run to do this. Running off the bike, for even ten minutes, is enough to prep your body for running after a bike. Why kill yourself to perform super-long runs after a bike?

BRICK WORKOUT PACING

Pacing is the final piece of the brick workout puzzle. Less is more in the case of brick workout pacing—and most triathletes go too hard, too often.

Remember when I said you don't need to run super long in the brick run because you're already building endurance with the long run? The same is true for how fast you run your brick runs. You're already working on speed in the intense run. Rarely does the brick run need to be completed at a fast pace.

The vast majority of the year, during the base building season and most of the strength building season, your brick runs should be done underneath your low heart rate cap that we calculated for the long run. This allows you to get in extra runs (with low impact on your body) keeping you fresh for the days when you actually need to push long or hard.

Towards the end of the strength and speed building season, and during the race season, you'll sprinkle in some efforts in your brick runs that are faster. By sprinkling, I mean that one brick run per week will have a small section that's at or above race pace.

For Sprint and Olympic distance triathletes, this faster section is a five to 10-minute section at the start of the run anywhere from 10-40 seconds faster per kilometer (16-64 seconds per mile) to teach your body how to deal with the excitement of coming out of transition, which most triathletes do a tad too hard, then settle into a more reasonable race pace.

For 70.3 and IRONMAN athletes, this section can be a fast five to 10-minute section at the start of a brick run, but in the three to four weeks immediately prior to a race, I'd rather your runs start out slow, building into a faster section at the end of the brick run. This pacing strategy is crucial to engrain into your body because if you go too hard out of transition in the longer distances, you're setting yourself up for a bonk later on. It's vital to hold your pacing back coming out of Transition 2.

Don't stress too much about brick workout pacing, as the purpose of the brick run is largely accomplished simply by the fact that you're running after a bike, and even at the slower paces most of your brick runs should be done at, the post-bike run is providing a big benefit. In the next part of this book, we'll talk about the intense run, where fast pacing very much is the focus. Let's make you fast now!

THE INTENSE RUN

Often for new triathletes, the goal is to just finish the race. Make it to the finish line, some way, somehow. With the long run and the brick run workouts in your wheelhouse, you'll develop the ability and confidence to finish your races strong and according to your game plan.

Then there'll come a time when merely finishing your race becomes old hat. Competitive juices will start flowing. How can I finish *faster?* How can I move up in my age category? How can I become a world champion? These sentences will no doubt cross your mind as you progress through the sport. And this is where speed comes into play. Remember: speed kills... the competition!

Unfortunately, more often than not when I look at athletes' placings in races they've done over several years, what I see is that they get a little better in their first few races because they become more familiar with triathlon, but quickly the progress tapers off and the athlete falls into a rut of working hard without a lot of payoff.

Typically, what I find the problem causing this stagnant performance is the fact that when triathletes try to run hard, they don't run hard enough. Runs tend to be a little bit hard and a little bit long; when athletes try to "tighten the screws" and push the pace, it tends to be during one of their normal runs and it's a small section where, for a few minutes, they bring up the pace by 10-15%. But this isn't enough of a difference in pace to make any progress, it's a good way to tire yourself out.

For my first two years in triathlon, I ran (jogged, really) two to three times per week. It tended to be the same route, roughly the same distance, and when a good song came on, or I felt extra badass, I'd pick up the pace for a while. But in the end, the routes always took me about the same time, give or take a couple minutes.

I'd show up to races thinking, "my running is feeling pretty good, I'm going to get off that bike and tear that run course apart!" But I'd get onto the run course and, race after race, it was the same thing: a suffer-fest at the same slow pace I'd always done.

In fact, the finish times from the two races below are from the 2010 Riding Mountain Olympic triathlon and the 2011 Riding Mountain Olympic triathlon. You can see that after an entire year of running and thinking I was putting in good training, I got slower.

2010

Men 25-29

Place	Total	Bib #	Competitor	City	Swim	Bike	Run
1	2:16:41	382	Les FRIESEN	Steinbach	28:08	1:10:37	37:57
2	2:34:36	388	Christopher SCHWEITZER	Regina	26:27	1:20:57	47:13
3	2:36:45	52	Mathieu BROSSEAU	Brandon	30:42	1:24:01	42:03
4	2:42:19	444	Scott BEATON	Winnipeg	26:05	1:24:47	51:28
5	3:04:58	409	Taren GESELL	Winnipeg	41:31	1:31:34	51:54

2011

Men 25 - 29

Place	Total	Bib #	Competitor	City	Swim	Bike	Run
1	2:09:13	40	Brendan MACKENZIE	Regina	23:50	1:07:26	37:57
2	2:15:49	98	Murray CARTER	St. Anne	28:15	1:07:52	39:43
3	2:26:08	76	Ryan LAMONT	Brandon	30:16	1:14:52	41:02
4	2:45:21	39	Todd HAMILTON	Winnipeg	32:56	1:22:31	49:55
5	2:52:14	42	Taren GESELL	Winnipeg	31:39	1:24:14	56:22
6	3:09:00	59	Steve LANGSTON	Winnipeg	39:04	1:26:35	1:03:22

In these two races in 2010 and 2011, I held average paces of 5:09/km (8:17/mile), and 5:38/km (9:03/mile). In 2011, I also completed my first regular half-marathon, which wasn't much better. I clocked a 1:52:13 for an average pace of 5:19/km (8:33/mile).

COMP.	VIEW	BIB	NAME	CATEGORY	RANK	GENDER PLACE	CAT. PLACE	OFFICIAL TIME
○	⊖	9602	Taren Gesell	M25-29	708	554	74	02:03:00.2

SPLIT NAME	SPLIT DISTANCE	SPLIT TIME	PACE	DISTANCE	RACE TIME	OVERALL (/3812)	GENDER (/1838)	CATEGORY (/211)	TIME OF DAY
SPLIT 1	12.8 km	01:03:52	4:59/km	12.8 km	01:03:52	475	395	59	
SPLIT 3	8.3 km	00:48:22	5:49/km	21.1 km	01:52:14	708	552	74	
CHIP TIME		01:52:13.8	5:19/km	21.1 km	01:52:13.8	708	552	74	
OFFICIAL TIME		02:03:00.2	5:49/km	21.1 km	02:03:00.2	1070	747	94	

But a really interesting thing happened after that disastrous late summer 2011 Olympic triathlon. Several months later, in the spring of 2012, I entered another half marathon with incredibly different results, going 1:36:57 for an average pace of 4:46/km (7:24/mile).

```
100  90/759  12/111  M5054  1920 Timothy Tapley    Winnipeg   1:36:56  4:36
101  91/759   8/73   M2529    72 Taren Gesell       Winnipeg   1:36:57  4:36
102  92/759   9/73   M2529    14 Reid Gallant       Winnipeg   1:37:01  4:36
```

Just five weeks later, I improved upon those times, doing another half marathon and going 1:32:39 for an average pace of 4:23/km (7:03/mile).

COMP.	VIEW	BIB	NAME	CATEGORY	RANK	GENDER PLACE	CAT. PLACE	OFFICIAL TIME
○	⊖	7322	Taren GESELL	M25-29	93	86	13	01:32:39.9

SPLIT NAME	SPLIT DISTANCE	SPLIT TIME	PACE	DISTANCE	RACE TIME	OVERALL (/3817)	GENDER (/1899)	CATEGORY (/235)	TIME OF DAY
SPLIT 1	9.6 km	00:40:37	4:13/km	9.6 km	00:40:37	104	99	18	
SPLIT 2	11.5 km	00:52:04	4:31/km	21.1 km	01:32:40	93	86	13	
OFFICIAL TIME		01:32:39.9	4:23/km	21.1 km	01:32:39.9	93	86	13	

And, in the very first triathlon of the year, I ended up running 20:40 for the 5K of the local Birds Hill Park Sprint triathlon, averaging 4:08/km (6:40/mile) on a very hilly, packed gravel course.

Male 30 to 34 Sprint

Rank	Name	Club	Time	Swim	Bike	Swim+Bike	Run
1	Kevin Earl	3rd Wave	01:20:32	00:12:53 (1)	00:46:28 (1)	00:59:21 (1)	00:21:11 (3)
2	Taren Gesell	Tri MB	01:22:37	00:14:45 (2)	00:47:11 (2)	01:01:56 (2)	00:20:40 (2)
3	John Power	TriFactor	01:26:23	00:17:31 (3)	00:48:26 (3)	01:05:57 (3)	00:20:26 (1)
4	Scott Kemp	Tri MB	01:40:38	00:17:53 (4)	00:57:14 (4)	01:15:08 (4)	00:25:30 (4)
5	Chris Fortier		01:41:53	00:18:28 (5)	00:57:30 (5)	01:15:58 (5)	00:25:55 (5)

All this improvement developed over one winter of training. You might be thinking that I must have hired a coach to figure out my training. Nope. Or, you may assume I lost a huge amount of weight. Not the case (in all fairness, I did lose about 15 pounds during that winter). Or, you could be thinking I changed my running technique, unlocking some magically faster stride. Guess again.

Over the course of the 2011- '12 winter, I changed exactly one thing: once a week, I ran fast. Really fast. When I was on the treadmill, I would crank it up to max speed and run for 10 or 20 seconds as hard as I could. I'd play with the incline on the treadmill and see how hard I could go before feeling like I was going to fall off. I went to a nearby soccer field and ran 50-yard wind sprints.

I didn't even do huge amounts of this, maybe 10 or 12 wind sprints, or eight 15-second hard intervals on the treadmill. I made sure that the effort was hard, as in, "Oh my god, I didn't think I'd EVER be able to go this fast" hard.

All other runs stayed the same. I didn't make my usual run route any longer or faster. I didn't hire a coach, or get run technique instruction. Literally, all I did was run really damn hard for a few seconds every week.

Studies[2] support that even for long distance IRONMAN athletes, fast efforts are just as important as building endurance. In a study of 61 IRONMAN athletes, one of the three factors that resulted in better performances in the race was VO2 Max, the maximum amount of oxygen that can be processed by an athlete. Higher VO2 Max is strongly correlated with faster times, and

---

[2] https://www.researchgate.net/publication/320514363_Maximal_Fat_Oxidation
_is_Related_to_Performance_in_an_IRONMAN_Triathlon

VO2 Max is best built with hard intervals ranging from 15 seconds to eight minutes.

This doesn't mean that you should go out and start knocking off as many hard efforts as you can possibly do before you throw up (or if you want to be extra cool at the track, go ahead and throw up). These hard runs took a lot out of me. By the end of that season, I developed scar tissue in my hamstring and a lower back imbalance that followed me around for the next six years before I figured out how to address it.

Hard and fast running is one of the best things you can do for your run training. It needs to be done properly so you don't develop a six-year injury that bugs you every time you ramp up your training.

In this section, we're going to tell you why hard running works so well, and how to structure it throughout a season for the best effectiveness.

WHY FAST RUNNING WORKS

In my *Triathlon Bike Foundations* book, we talked at length about High Intensity Interval Training (HIIT) and the principle of hormesis. HIIT training is commonly associated with bike intervals in things such as trainer rides, spin classes, or even your weekly hard group rides. But the same benefits and principles apply to running.

Hormesis is a process where your body is exposed to a small dose of a stress, that if given in larger doses, could severely harm you. In response, the body sees the stress as a potential threat and adapts. If the stress returns in the future, the body is prepared for it. Vaccines are a form of a hormetic stress: you're injected with a small dose of a disease, and the body creates antibodies to fight the disease in case a larger, more harmful dose of the disease comes.

The thing about hormesis that works well for us athletes is that the body doesn't only adapt to be strong enough to fight the dose that we received originally. The body says, "I'm going to get so much stronger so that if this jerk is ever going to put me through something like that again, I'll be way stronger than whatever that junk was."

Where this comes into play with your training is when you want to get faster or stronger. If you push yourself a little bit harder than is comfortable or than you thought you were able, your body will adapt. You'll become faster and stronger. Push a little bit more and you'll get faster yet. Repeat this cycle over and over, constantly performing exercises that are a little faster, longer, with shorter rest between intervals, and you'll gradually turn into a faster athlete. Pairing these hard efforts with at least seven hours a night of sleep, and good healthful foods, is indeed a recipe for success.

Intense training has a huge number of other benefits beyond only making you faster and stronger:

- Intense training stimulates hormonal health, combating some of the hormonal challenges common to endurance athletes.
- It stimulates the recruitment of more muscle fibers so that we can access more of our muscle fibers even at lower intensities.
- It can burn fat for up to 48 hours after the workout is complete by a process called Post Exercise Oxygen Consumption.
- It increases your VO2 Max, the measurement most commonly associated with increased fitness, so that you can process more oxygen each minute.
- It decreases how much pain you feel during exercise so that all effort levels feel easier.
- It increases endurance as much, if not more, as moderate intensity training. In some studies, just one minute of hard exercise each week was as effective at increasing endurance as several hours of moderate intensity training.
- It offers a massive training effect in a minimal amount of time. This is tremendously valuable for age group triathletes who are tight on time.

You can read *The One-Minute Workout* from *Triathlon Taren Podcast* guest Dr. Martin Gibala to understand the full benefits and mechanisms involved in HIIT training. Or, if you really want to dive into the specific application of HIIT for triathletes, you can enroll in HIIT Science for Triathlon, taught by Dr. Paul Laursen, accompanied by Dr. Dan Plews, (both of whom I've personally worked with, been coached by, and have had on our podcast), which talks about exactly how to use HIIT for triathlon training.

For now, all you need to know is that pushing hard (really hard) has huge benefits, not just for your triathlon swimming, biking and running performance, but for your overall health.

How *hard* is hard? Generally, hard means pushing your rate of perceived exertion levels, on a scale of one to ten, between eight and 10 for anywhere between 15 seconds to eight minutes. Specifically, I recommend going to mymottiv.com/runfoundations and downloading our Zone Calculator which will tailor training zones based off heart rate and perceived exertion for you; for HIIT training we're talking about Zones 4 and 5.

When I made that huge jump in run performance many years ago, the results were almost instant—but the progress was short lived. I made improvements by leaps and bounds because of these benefits of HIIT training. But because I didn't know how to structure a training season, or set up training so that progress could be made year after year, I stalled on making progress for several years. We're now going to get into how to set up your once-per-week intense run so you can make progress over the course of a year (and every year) by constantly giving your body stress and rest at the right times, in the right ways.

Use the following guidelines to periodize your one hard run each week throughout the training season.

HARD HILL SPRINTS

Some of my favourite hard run workouts are the ones at the start of the year. These are the hard hill sprints done after a restful off-season. On the MōTTIV training app, the off-season for most athletes ends in the middle of November when we enter base build season and start making training more structured. We also start adding small little bursts of intensity with long rest times between. This mid-November to end-of-December time frame is the perfect moment to include some hard hill sprints.

Run coach legend Bobby McGee is a huge believer that the number one factor dictating an elite runner's ability to run well is weekly high mileage, getting into the 100-plus miles per week range (note: he's talking about runners specifically, not triathletes.) Yet, even Bobby McGee is a huge proponent of starting the season with hard hill sprints.

Hard hill sprints are a great way to kickstart the season because they have a number of benefits that carry through into the race season:

- Hill running encourages good form with a forward lean, an upright posture and getting up on the balls of your feet.
- It encourages a forceful arm drive that encourages a stronger leg stride.
- It forces the body to recruit as many muscle fibers as possible for the running motion (would you rather run being able to only access 60% of your running muscle groups, or 90% of your running muscle groups?)
- It's sport-specific strength building. While deadlifts and plyometrics are great for building overall body strength, they don't translate to running strength and speed without doing a very run-specific strength movement. Hill running is that sport-specific movement.

Personally, I find these short intense hill sessions a lot of fun, too. They're super intense and challenging, but they're short enough that just when things are getting tough, you're done. Here's how to do these intense hill sprints.

If you're following the typical triathlon season, you'll start introducing harder training intervals after you've rested up from the previous season, or you'll start training in a structured fashion for your first season towards the middle and end of November.

When you start introducing intervals, you'll want them to be short, slightly intense, low volume, with long rests in between.

At the onset of your structured training, a harder run session might look something like this for two or three weeks as your body adjusts to hill running:

> ➢ 30-minute run staying mostly in a low heart rate training zone.
>
> ➢ During this run, include six, 8- to 10-second harder intervals when you're going up a hill with a rate of perceived exertion of 7-8/10.
>
> ➢ The hill incline should be steep, but not incredibly steep. In the next phase, we'll increase the incline of the hill to as steep as possible while still being able to run. This incline is slightly less intense than that.
>
> ➢ Make sure to have a few minutes rest between the intervals to fully recover.
>
> ➢ When running the harder sections, focus on driving your arms forcefully and staying upright. The hill will almost force the rest of your body into good running technique.

After two to three weeks, your body will be better adapted to hill running and you can include more structured and harder intervals. A workout during this time looks like this:

> ➢ 30-minute run staying mostly in a low heart rate training zone.
>
> ➢ During this run, include six 8-second max effort intervals when you're going up a hill with a rate of perceived exertion of 9 to 10 out of 10.

> ➤ The hill incline should be as steep as possible while still being able to run up the hill. We're going for a fast run, not a fast walk or hike.
> ➤ Take 2-3 minutes rest between the intervals.
> ➤ When running the harder sections, focus on driving your arms forcefully and staying upright, the hill will almost force the rest of your body into good running technique.

These short, maximum-effort hill intervals are great to do all the way through December (and even a little bit into January). As you progress week by week, you can extend the interval from eight seconds to nine or 10 seconds, increase the number of intervals from six up to 10 intervals, or reduce the rest period from two or three minutes down to a minute.

Remember, as you're changing the workout and progressing it slightly, more isn't always better. A handful of these short burst intervals have a huge training effect. Doing 20 of these, or making them 30 seconds long, is getting away from their main benefit, which is to push to a MAX MAX MAX effort for a short period of time, recruiting a bunch of muscle fibers.

See what I mean when I say short but hard? Anyone can do six hard efforts for eight seconds. Go for it and don't hold back!

LONG HILL INTERVALS

As you get into January and February, you'll want to transition away from these ultra-short intervals into some longer grinding hill reps that are still quite intense, but not quite as eye-poppingly so.

Because your body will now be adapted to the act of hill running and intensity, you won't need an adjustment period to adapt to the hills. Your first longer hill rep workouts can look like this:

> ➢ 30-minute run staying mostly in a low heart rate training zone.
> ➢ During this run, include at least a five-minute easy warm up and cool down.
> ➢ Also include six one-minute hard effort hill reps at a rate of perceived exertion of 8 to 9 out of 10.
> ➢ The hill incline should be steep, but not as steep as the max effort hill reps as we're looking to encourage fast foot speed. Somewhere in an 8-10% grade is appropriate.
> ➢ Take two to three minutes rest between the intervals
> ➢ When running the harder sections, focus on driving your arms forcefully, staying upright, working on fast foot speed

If you're a Sprint or Olympic distance triathlete, you don't need to extend the total duration of this run, but you can increase the length of the hill interval and decrease the rest time. As you get toward the end of February or early March, a workout could look like this:

> ➤ 30-minute run staying mostly in a low heart rate training zone.
>
> ➤ During this run, include at least a five-minute easy warm up and cool down.
>
> ➤ Also include six two-minute hard effort hill reps at a rate of perceived exertion of 8 to 9 out of 10.
>
> ➤ The hill incline should be steep, but not as steep as the max effort hill reps as we're looking to encourage fast foot speed. Somewhere in an 8-10% grade is appropriate.
>
> ➤ Take one to two minutes rest between the intervals.
>
> ➤ When running the harder sections, focus on driving your arms forcefully, staying upright, working on fast foot speed.

If you're a 70.3 or IRONMAN distance triathlete, you'll want to extend the total run time, the duration of the hill intervals, decrease the rest period and increase the number of intervals. As you get towards the end of February or early March, a workout could look like this:

- ➢ 40-minute run staying mostly in a low-heart-rate training zone.
- ➢ During this run, include at least a five-minute easy warm up and cool down.
- ➢ Also include eight two-minute hard effort hill reps at a rate of perceived exertion of 8 to 9 out of 10.
- ➢ The hill incline should be steep but not as steep as the max effort hill reps as we're looking to encourage fast foot speed. Somewhere in an 8-10% grade is appropriate.
- ➢ Take one to two minutes rest between the intervals.
- ➢ When running the harder sections focus on driving your arms forcefully, staying upright, working on fast foot speed.

Now that you've gone through over three months of harder interval-based training with a serious focus on strong forceful running on hills, your arms will be trained to drive forcefully and encourage quick foot turnover on flat roads. Your body posture, strong and upright. Your leg drive, powerful. You'll have access to as many of the muscle groups in your legs as possible. Your overall running form will be excellent.

At this point, we will transition away from doing your hard intervals on hills, to doing them on flat land so you can translate that excellent running power into excellent running speed. Remember that during the race season, you'll maintain some occasional hill running during your less intense long runs so you maintain the excellent benefits that hill running offers.

SHORT INTERVALS

The next progression in your weekly speed building fast run workout is short intervals. These can start toward the end of February. The first thing to know about these harder intervals on flat land (whether they're long or short) is that they're tough on the body and can lead to injury. That's why we start you off with hill intervals at the beginning of the season. They're easier on the body and provide a good way to get training benefits while adapting to harder work in a safe manner.

If there's a single workout that's likely to injure you more than all others, it's these fast interval workouts on the track or on pavement. There are a few rules you should follow to reduce the likelihood of injury:

After a run, always use foam rollers and trigger point balls to work out tight knots and niggles

If you start a fast run, and after the warm-up you still feel a nagging injury that's causing you pain, pull the plug and don't do that run. If it's a minor injury, it will loosen up and feel better by the end of a warm-up

If you have an injury that's causing pain for several days after a run, and up to three weeks or more, go see a physiotherapist who specializes in treating athletes

These short intervals can be done on a track with distance intervals, or on a treadmill or road with time intervals (also known as fartleks). In a perfect world, you're able to do these on a rubber surface or dirt track because intervals are hard on the body and the track helps reduce that pounding and likelihood of injury. The treadmill is less desirable for these fast intervals. When you get good at treadmill running, you can cheat by running in more of a bouncing stride instead of a stride that drives you forward.

Even though you may have built up to max-effort eight-second hill sprints, and longer two-minute near max-effort hill sprints, you'll want to start out your short interval workouts on flat land very gradually. This means that when you start doing short intervals on flat land, they'll be a little shorter than what you built up to and a little less intense. We'll then gradually build up intensity and duration.

During these short intervals, we'll keep the rest intervals long so you can get a full recovery. As we progress into the race season and longer intervals, that's when we'll start shortening the rest interval to make the workouts more similar to a race situation.

For the first two or three weeks, adjust to these flat land intervals with a workout that looks like this:

- ➤ 10-minute easy jog.
- ➤ Five minutes of dynamic stretching and strides to prime the body for the hard work to come.
- ➤ 10x30 seconds (or 200 meters, if on a track) at fast, Zone 4 effort with a rate of perceived exertion around 8 to 9 out of 10.
- ➤ Easy jog for two minutes between intervals.
- ➤ 10-minute easy jog cool down.

Add it up and see we're still just doing five total minutes of hard running in this workout—and that's some of the hardest running you'll do all week. Only five minutes of being a badass is enough to make huge gains.

When athletes on the MōTTIV training app ask me how hard should these hard intervals be, my answer is that they should be the fastest pace you can possibly hold, but not so fast that you a) can't hold that exact same pace over all the intervals and b) don't end the workout feeling like you could have done another interval at that same pace. I want you to run as fast as possible, at the same pace over all the intervals, and finish feeling like you could have done one more.

After this three-week period of adjusting to harder workouts on flat land, you'll be ready to increase the duration and intensity of this hard run. Gradually increase the duration of the intervals and bring up the intensity until workouts look like this by the end of April:

- ➤ 10-minute easy jog.
- ➤ Five minutes of dynamic stretching and strides to prime the body for the hard work to come.
- ➤ 3-5x4 minutes (or 800 meters, if on a track) at max sustainable effort, with a rate of perceived exertion around 9 out of 10.
- ➤ Easy jog for three to four minutes between intervals so that you're fully recovered.
- ➤ **Sprint and Olympic distance athletes:** perform three to four of these intervals.
- ➤ **70.3 and IRONMAN athletes** should perform four to five of these intervals, based on how good you're feeling in the final interval and what your schedule allows.
- ➤ 10-minute easy jog cool down.

At this point, you'll have built up a huge amount of raw running speed and strength from the hill intervals. You'll also have transferred that ability onto flat land so that you've got a higher VO2 Max and better foot speed. Now the work will transition into longer intervals. We'll refine that work into the ability to hold that higher speed for longer and longer periods of time, so you can be fast on race day.

LONG INTERVALS

Once you've done the hill work to increase running strength and power, translating those abilities into raw speed with some fast work on the track or road, it's time to sharpen your run speed so you can run well for a sustained period of time. We do this with long intervals and tempo runs.

Long interval running is in the four to eight-minute effort range. While 15- to 30-second intervals initially help increase VO2 Max and your ability to process more oxygen each minute, you need to extend that VO2 Max to longer durations so you can sustain the high efforts over the longer duration of a race. Four minutes is still a great VO2 Max interval, six minutes is still good, while eight minutes is about the longest interval you'll do while still being able to go hard enough to work on your VO2 Max.

For the first few weeks of doing these longer intervals, as we've done with the previous types of intense run workouts, you'll want to ease into them to adjust to the new workout. You'll design your workouts with a little longer rest, intensity will be slightly down and number of intervals will be lower.

This is a workout I did along with pro triathletes Lucy and Reece Charles-Barclay, at the beginning of a period of working on VO2 Max long intervals:

> ➢ 10-minute easy jog.
> ➢ Five minutes of dynamic stretching and strides to warm up.
> ➢ 5x1 km at 8 - 9 out of 10 rate of perceived exertion.
> ➢ Pace goal was to run hard, but not have any major time difference between the first and last interval, and to end feeling like we could have done more.
> ➢ Reece average pace: 3:03/km (4:54/mile).
> ➢ Lucy average pace: 3:12/km (5:09/mile).
> ➢ Taren average pace: 3:30/km (5:38/mile).
> ➢ Four-minute easy jog, walk rest between intervals.
> ➢ 10-minute easy jog cool down.

You can see that the interval times are short, under the four-minute guidelines. And the rest interval is longer than the hard interval. We also only did five of these kilometers. Sprint and Olympic distance athletes would be good doing two or three intervals, respectively.

As the race season progresses, the interval gets longer. More intervals get completed, and the rest interval shrinks. By the end of my season, this was a workout I did prior to 2019 Challenge Roth:

> ➢ 10-minute easy jog.
> ➢ Five minutes of dynamic stretching and strides to warm up.
> ➢ 8x1 mile at 8 out of 10 rate of perceived exertion.

➢ Pace goal was to run hard, but not have any major time difference between the first and last interval, and to end feeling like I could have done one more. My average pace: 3:50/km (6:10/mile).

➢ One-minute easy jog rest between intervals.

➢ 10-minute easy jog cool down.

As you progress throughout the season, feel free to manipulate the workout however you feel you want. It doesn't need to be a straight linear progression from 4-minute intervals to 4.5 minutes, to 5, to 5.5, and so on. For one, three-week block you can do 6x4 minute intervals, while in the next three week block you can do 3x8 minutes. Here are some guidelines for how to design this intense run workout:

➢ Sprint and Olympic athletes should target a total of 10-20 minutes of intense running during the workout.

➢ 70.3 and IRONMAN athletes should target a total of 20-35 minutes of intense running during the workout.

➢ As you get more comfortable with the intervals, gradually decrease rest time to as little as 60 seconds.

*The work-to-rest ratio should be roughly 4:1 (i.e., if you do four minutes hard, take a one-minute rest; if you do eight minutes hard, do two minutes rest.)

These hard intervals, done on a tight rest period, will astound you with how hard you're able to continuously run. You'll unlock run speed in your races that you never thought possible.

In 2019, the first series of a big handful of intervals I did were 6x1 km with a one-minute rest. I barely averaged 4:00/km (6:26/mile) and I thought I was going to throw up during the last couple. Within a couple months, I was able to do 30-40 minutes straight holding 4:05/km (6:34/mile) and it felt easy. Remember, the workouts in this part of the season aren't necessarily about increasing speed. It's about holding speed for longer periods of time.

By the time my final race of 2019 came around, IM Atlantic City 70.3, the "in a perfect world target run pace" I used in 70.3s of 4:30 per km seemed so easy that I was able to hold an average pace of 4:27/km despite dehydration and blood pressure issues that were causing me to feel cold on the run despite it being 81 degrees Fahrenheit with 80% humidity. Run these hard intervals regularly and you'll be amazed at what you're able to do come race day.

There's one last fast run you need to do to sharpen up for your race. While you can certainly keep with these super hard runs right up to your taper, I'd encourage you to switch to a tempo run in the final three weeks before your taper to get a good sense of what a sustainable fast pace is.

A tempo run is a run that's uncomfortably hard, but sustainable for a long duration of time. For example, my tempo runs prior to 2019 Challenge Roth were 60 minutes at 4:30/km while my target race pace was 5:00/km. My tempo runs prior to IM 70.3 Atlantic City 2019 were 30 minutes at 4:05/km, while my target run pace was 4:25/km.

You're looking to do a continuous run at a faster pace than your goal race pace. This will sharpen up your ability to run fast for the race. Here are some guidelines:

➤ Sprint tempo runs should be 15 minutes long.

➤ Olympic tempo runs should be 20 minutes long.

➤ 70.3 tempo runs should be 30 minutes long.

➤ IRONMAN tempo runs should be 60 minutes long.

➤ Pace per kilometer should be anywhere from 15 seconds faster than your target average race pace to 35 seconds faster than your target average race pace. It should be slightly uncomfortable, but manageable for the duration of the long tempo interval.

Do this tempo run a couple times in the final three weeks before your taper starts, then include some of this tempo pace (albeit for a shorter duration) during your taper, and you will have the power, the strength, the speed, the foot turnover and the endurance to hold all that running talent for the length of your race. You'll get into the race and if you've done all the work, you'll be so well prepared for the run that it might almost feel easy.

PERIODIZE AND PRIORITIZE THROUGHOUT THE SEASON

The guidelines above, which take you from super short hill running, to longer hill running, to short intervals and eventually into long sustained intervals are what's called periodization. Doing only the same exercises year-round will cause your body to adapt and you'll stop getting benefits from the workouts. Plus, there's only a certain amount of time your body can hold peak race fitness.

There are a couple of other things to note about managing a season to make sure you get as fast and fit as possible, while still staying healthy and injury free.

If you're new to triathlon training, you should take a rest week every third week. You can still do some intense running, but reduce the number of intervals to half of what you did during the previous week. For example, take a look at this basic three-week schedule:

- **Week 1**: 10x30sec hard
- **Week 2**: 10x30sec hard, trying to be a little faster than the previous week
- **Week 3 (Rest)**: 5x30sec hard, going a little easier than your pace in the previous two weeks

No one (not even the pros, whose lives revolve around their training, or me, whose life revolves around triathlon) can nail every single workout throughout the year, or heck, even throughout an entire three-week cycle. There are some times throughout the year when you can forget about the intense run if it isn't working well. Here are some pointers:

- If you're feeling injured or over-trained, don't bother with the intense run
- During the base building season of November and December, if you're busy, you can make the intense run optional
- During race season, try your best to always fit in the intense run as long as you feel healthy (no sicknesses or injuries)

Remember, no one's a machine. Even the people online who appear to be actual machines have rough days too—and many of them who brag about pushing through fatigue, injury or busy schedules by getting up at 4 a.m., often end up over-trained and injured through nobody's fault but their own (they often won't admit to it publicly, anyway). If you feel sick, stressed, busy or injured, it's OK to miss a day here and there. Don't stress about it. If you're able to hit around 80% of your workouts bang on, week after week, year after year, you'll be plenty fit, making progress every single season.

All this might feel like it's a lot to put together. I remember when I read my very first triathlon training book, *The Triathlete's Training Bible* by Joe Friel. I can look back on it now and say it's a fantastic book. But when I first read it, although I knew I was learning something, I had no idea how to implement what the book had just told me. This is normal, and I recognize that might even be what happens when people read our books, watch our YouTube videos, or listen to our podcasts. It's one thing to read about a system but it's a whole other thing to implement it, so if you ever feel like you can't piece it all together, go check out the MōTTIV training app, which automates our entire training system and methodology.

That is where you can get your training periodized throughout an entire year, including swim, bike, run, yoga and strength workouts (in-season and off-season) with advice on the required nutrition for each workout, and a community of awesome people to train with and motivate each other right at your fingertips. Feel free to check out a free trial of the MōTTIV training app at app.mymottiv.com.

CHAPTER 3

TRIATHLON RUNNING TECHNIQUE

The first year that I was in triathlon, I woke up every morning feeling like I had lost a hammer fight. My joints ached, my lower back was sore, I developed shin splints, my feet were always sore. You know those people who say things like, "I'm just not built for running," or "I can't run because every time I do, I get injured"? I was that person.

Everything hurt when I ran, and it hurt even more the next morning. I felt I must be too thick to run like those effortless-looking runners you see in track and field events. When I went into my first few triathlons, things didn't magically get better.

Yet, as of writing this in 2019, I've clocked a 3:24 IRONMAN marathon, and I recently held a personal best 70.3 half marathon pace of 4:27/km at 2019 IM 70.3 Atlantic City.

I didn't make this progress by becoming a great runner. When you look at my running technique, it still looks pretty forced. When I go a couple of weeks without running, like in the off-season, I come back feeling like an aluminum folding lawn chair that got rusted from being left out in the rain. The great thing about triathlon, though, is that we don't need to become world class swimmers, cyclists or runners to do well in the sport. We just need a basic level of proficiency.

That big, long, butt-kicking running stride, where track and elite marathon runners are up on their toes, prancing effortlessly across the running course, isn't necessary for us age-group triathletes for a couple reasons.

First, the speeds we run at aren't fast enough to require that elite-runner technique. Even the fastest runners in our sport are as much as 20% slower than elite runners. And we amateurs are 100%, or even 200%, slower than elite runners—even if we're good triathlon runners. A four-hour marathon in an IRONMAN is quite a good run, but it's nowhere near what's required of elite runners.

Second, running in triathlon has a different load on the body than pure running. We have to run when we're already tired after a swim and a bike. We have to run when our body is lacking energy. Elite runners can start their runs fresh, with all the carbohydrate stores in the world, which allows them to run to their body's full potential. Triathletes need to race their entire run in preservation mode. We start our runs tired, needing to conserve as many calories as possible.

You need to forget a lot of what you learned from running coaches, running drills, running magazines and running-specific thought leaders. It's not relevant to triathlon running. The great thing about this is that you don't need to become an amazing runner. You need to develop very simple run technique that's easy for (usually) stiff amateur triathletes to perform, allowing you to run well for the entire race.

In the next part of this book, we're going to dispel some triathlon run myths you've maybe heard in the past. Once that's cleared up, we'll get to how to run well in triathlon.

TRIATHLON RUNNING IS JUST LIKE RUNNING

The first myth is that triathlon running is just like all other running. This isn't really a myth, but it's something that's been overlooked. Running in a pure running race is about running fast, while running in triathlon is about conserving energy and running fast as a result, because you can run without slowing down or stopping all the way to the end of the race. Let's look at a couple different points of technique to show how different running and triathlon running are.

Elite track and marathon runners have big leg kicks that go up so high, they almost kick themselves in the butt. Go into the running technique videos at mymottiv.com/runfoundations and look at footage of Patrick Lange, one of the fastest runners in triathlon and a two-time IRONMAN World Champion, and even though he's doing 3:40/km (5:53/mile) his feet stay fairly low to the ground.

Next, elite runners tend to have fairly big arm swings with low shoulders to drive their legs fast and forcefully. Go to mymottiv.com/runfoundations and look at the running footage from Anne Haug, 2019 IRONMAN World Champion and probably the best runner in the female long distance triathlon game. See how high her shoulders are, how her arms are tucked up high and how little her arms move (it's definitely not a full arm swing).

Check out running footage on YouTube of Mario Mola and Javier Gomez. They're running much faster than anyone in IRONMAN, and even at a speed of a 15 minute/5 km, their feet are lower to the ground, their shoulders are higher and their arms aren't pumping as much as elite runners in track or marathon events.

Put aside those running technique books written by run coaches, be cautious of anyone telling you to run a certain way because that's "good run technique," and rest assured that if you focus on efficient triathlon running (which is much easier to achieve) you'll soon be running well.

FOREFOOT RUNNING IS THE ONLY WAY TO RUN

Along with the barefoot running movement came the forefoot running movement. This is the belief that the best way to run is by landing on your forefoot, which is the front or the ball of your foot. If you were to take off your shoes and run barefoot, you'd naturally land more toward the front of your foot, and the impact on the ground would be softer, so people thought this was the best way to run.

But this is a little bit like *broscience*, where people reach conclusions based on what makes a good argument and not actual science. Take a look at elite marathon and track runners, and you'll see a mixture of runners who land on their heel, on their mid-foot or on their forefoot. Look at Daniela Ryf, one of the best triathlon runners in the world, and you'll see she lands on her heel. Chrissie Wellington, Patrick Lange, Gwen Jorgensen and a huge number of other great triathlon runners land on their heels. So, what gives?

Instead of coming to a conclusion based on what seems logical, we need to look at actual evidence, and there's evidence that shows when running at any pace slower than a 4:00/km (6:26/mile) pace, landing on your heel is more efficient.[3]

So, does this mean you should land on your heel? No. It means that the belief that you *HAVE TO* land on your mid or forefoot first is baloney. In the next chapter, we'll discuss how you should land with your foot.

THE HIGHER THE CADENCE THE BETTER

Running cadence is the number of steps you take each minute (strides per minute, or SPM). Triathletes often hear, "You've got to increase your running cadence," without any guideline for how or why to increase running cadence. The magical number triathletes often hear is that they have to run at a minimum of 180 steps per minute—and that higher is always better. Again, this isn't true.

Higher cadence is more efficient and uses less oxygen as demonstrated in a 2019 study[4] showing that, after just 10 days of high cadence training, the runners used 11% less oxygen at the same pace. This is huge, but this doesn't mean higher is *always* better.

---

[3] https://www.ncbi.nlm.nih.gov/pubmed/24002340

[4] https://www.ncbi.nlm.nih.gov/pubmed/31306391

As we've discussed, you're likely to cause injury if you force your body to run in an unnatural way. Some people have a lower natural running cadence. If you're injured, you won't be very fast—no matter how high your cadence is.

In my opinion, 180 SPM is the sweet spot. It's a running cadence that's not too quick, and is attainable for most people. Once you've reached a cadence of over 170, however, don't force yourself unnaturally to keep increasing that number.

Finally, unless you always run on very hilly or varying surfaces, try to keep your cadence the same at different paces and terrains to save your muscles from getting damaged in a race. If 90% of your running is at 175 SPM and then you go to hills and uneven terrain, and your cadence starts varying between 155 on uphills and 190 on downhills, that different movement pattern is going to take a lot out of your legs, because they aren't conditioned well for that different cadence.

It's natural to have a slower cadence for warming up or super intense running. For the most part, though, your running cadence shouldn't vary much.

STICK YOUR CHEST OUT, RUN TALL AND LEAN FORWARD

Sticking your chest out, running tall and leaning forward are great aspects of good running technique. But following this philosophy too literally could actually lead to runners developing bad technique.

You do want to have your chest slightly proud, be upright and have a slight lean forward. Absolutely. But the description "stick your chest out, run tall and lean forward" leads people to literally stick their chests out, locking their arms in place, running tall, over-extending their backs and leaning forward, causing a bit of a hunch.

I'd ignore these guidelines, or at the very least, ignore the description. We'll discuss proper upper body run technique in the next section, and there's an entire video demonstration about it at mymottiv.com/runfoundations.

THERE IS AN IDEAL RUN TECHNIQUE

It might seem kind of weird to be reading an entire section of a book dedicated to run technique, then in that same section read that there isn't a perfect run technique. Bear with me. I'm going somewhere promising with this.

Go to mymottiv.com/runfoundations and look at the running techniques of Mark Allen and Dave Scott during the Iron War at the 1989 IRONMAN World Championship. Mark Allen is a perfect runner, with a slight lean forward, legs tracking perfectly straight and arms pumping. I could watch it all day. Then look at Dave Scott. His run style is incredibly unconventional, yet he's one of the best IRONMAN triathletes to ever set foot on a course.

Next, I want you to look at the footage of Mirinda Carfrae, Chrissie Wellington and Daniela Ryf. Mirinda Carfrae is a snappy runner who has run down deficits so large, the world had written her off in the race. Now look at Chrissie Wellington and Daniela Ryf. Chrissie Wellington has a shuffle and is a little knock-kneed while running. Daniela Ryf is unsymmetrical, with a bit of a chicken-wing crossover with one arm.

The reason I'm getting you to look at these different running techniques isn't to show you what to do versus what not to do. It's because each of these athletes has run a marathon at IRONMAN Kona that's one of the 10 fastest marathon splits ever run in Kona. That's right: the flailing style of Dave Scott lead to the fourth fastest marathon ever run in Kona (second fastest, really, because when Dave ran this record-setting run, the total marathon time included transition). And while Mirinda Carfrae has the first, second and third fastest marathon times ever run in Kona, Chrissie Wellington has the fourth, and even unsymmetrical Daniela Ryf with her crossover arm has the tenth fastest marathon ever run in Kona.

It's unlikely you or I will ever look as effortless as Mark Allen or Mirinda Carfrae while running, but what I'm getting at is that it's OK if we don't look like that. In fact, it's probably a good thing we don't. That track-runner style of running is, as we've already discussed, inefficient over a long distance because it uses a lot of energy.

The run technique tips you're getting in the following section will give you the guidelines for how to develop an efficient and energy-saving run technique that reduces injury and will allow you to run strong until the end of the race. How you end up applying those run technique items is unique to everyone, based on your biomechanics and body structure. Don't stress about not looking the way you think you need to look while running. Everyone will look different, even if you've got the technique down pat.

Let's get into developing your own personal efficient triathlon running technique.

In this section, we're going to guide you into an efficient triathlon running technique. This isn't going to be the springy, huge leg stride technique you see elite runners do around a track, because that doesn't help us a lot in triathlon. And, frankly, we age group triathletes aren't flexible enough for that big running stride.

Instead, what you're going to be able to do after this chapter is use a running technique that isn't limited by your biomechanics or flexibility. The triathlon running technique will also save you energy and reduce muscle damage so it's not as hard on the body after a tiring bike, and it doesn't beat you up throughout the entire run leading to a high chance that you'll have to walk during the race.

You might wonder if this will hurt all your other running races, like the 5K or half-marathon events. Don't worry, this technique won't hold you back. Daniela Ryf, Anne Haug, Patrick Lange, and hundreds of fast triathletes use these techniques, and they're plenty fast. The only limitation: if you're trying to become an All-American track superstar, this might not be the run technique for you. But for us amateurs, it's exactly what we need.

Rather than kill a whole bunch of trees with dozens of photos in this section, I've recorded demonstration videos to show what I'm talking about in the techniques listed below. Go to mymottiv.com/runfoundations to follow along with the technique points below. Without seeing those videos, a lot of what I'm about to recommend won't make sense, or you'll miss some of the critical nuances of each technique item.

Don't try to change every last aspect of your triathlon running technique all at once, either, as you'll end up not doing anything well. Try to focus on changing one thing at a time, every four to six weeks until it feels more natural to run with the new method than it does with the old one.

A great way to start solidifying new running techniques is to start a run with your new method for about 50 meters, then switch to the old technique for 50 meters. Go back and forth for the first few minutes. This will help you feel the new method when you're warmed up and into your run. Let's start making those changes.

FEET

As we talked about in the last chapter, it doesn't matter if you land first on your heel, your mid-foot or your forefoot. Run naturally. Don't try to change it. When pro triathlete Josh Amberger was on our podcast, he said he went back to his more natural heel strike and a lot of his running injuries went away (he believed those injuries were caused by forcing himself to run with an unnatural mid-foot strike).

What's most important is where you land and place the most amount of your weight. You don't want to land and have weight bearing on your body out front of your center of mass. You want it roughly straight underneath your body.

It's OK to touch the ground first with your heel slightly out front of your body, then roll onto your foot, gradually bearing weight on it as you move forward, with your foot underneath your center of mass (this is how Daniela Ryf runs).

One drill you can use to learn how to feel where you should land is to hop up-and-down in place, transitioning to hopping from one foot to the other doing a butt kick, then lean forward.

You'll naturally take your first few steps directly underneath your center of mass. This is where you want to think about landing while you're running.

LEG SWING

The leg swing is a major deviation between elite runners and triathletes. You'll see elite runners with a huge circular leg motion, where their knee drives high, their foot extends out, and then after they push forward, their foot goes so far back and up that they almost kick themselves on the bum.

For triathletes, this huge leg movement uses a ton of energy, which isn't a big deal if you're running a 13-minute race, or even a two-hour marathon that you start with 100% fresh legs. But legs are huge muscle groups, and this motion uses a large amount of energy—energy that we don't have as triathletes, because we're starting the run already tired.

This huge leg movement also isn't necessarily possible for most age group triathletes who have tight hips, inactive glutes and nowhere near the range of motion as young, gazelle-like twenty-somethings. We (older) amateur triathletes need a much more efficient, easy-to-execute running stride.

The leg swing that's most efficient for triathletes is one with a small amount of movement in the upper leg and a closer to the ground sweeping movement with the lower leg. At mymottiv.com/runfoundations, the side angle video of Patrick Lange running is great to watch for an example of this technique.

Even though Patrick Lange was running at a pretty fast pace around 3:40/km (5:53/mile), his upper leg isn't moving a huge amount, and his feet stay pretty close to the ground, coming nowhere near kicking his butt like you'll see elite runners doing on the track.

What you're looking to do with your running stride is to sweep your foot close to the ground, pushing yourself forward, as opposed to bouncing up and down. Bouncing up and down will create muscle damage

As you're running, think about your leg like a pendulum that swings close to the ground with a small knee bend as opposed to a big spring with a huge knee bend.

HIPS & GLUTES

Go to any running race or triathlon and you'll see many runners sashaying back and forth like race walkers. This is a huge problem for all runners, but triathletes especially.

Most triathletes are regular age group adults who work normal jobs at a desk, drive around every day, sit and watch TV to unwind and spend their free time swimming, biking and running straight ahead. That's a recipe for inefficient running. All of that sitting shortens the front of the hip and makes the side stabilizing glutes go to sleep. Swimming, biking and running in a straight line doesn't make this any better because we don't do any lateral, side-to-side movements.

The side stabilizer muscles tend to be tremendously weak in most triathletes. And even if we don't look like those swaying race walkers, we tend to have little side-to-side movements in our body each time we land while running. This is "energy leakage" as top strength coach Erin Carson from ECFIT Strength in Boulder calls it. Instead of directing energy straight forward toward the finish line, we're sending energy out the side of our bodies, making us slower and potentially causing injury as our bodies try to stabilize themselves to move forward.

One way to correct this energy leakage is to be conscious of your hips and glutes. You want to focus on having a stable pelvic area that doesn't twist side-to-side or collapse with each foot stride. You also want to focus on pushing straight backward with your leg using your big, strong glute muscle.

The Shopping Cart Drill is best seen in the video demonstration at mymottiv.com/runfoundations and it will help you stabilize your hips and learn how to push yourself forward with one of the most powerful muscles in your body: your glutes.

If you're anti-video, the Shopping Cart Drill is basically as it sounds. Before you start a run, spend 30 seconds slowly walking as if you're pushing a shopping cart. Have your arms positioned like you would running, and with one very slow step every two seconds, push yourself forward, driving your leg behind you, activating your butt. Keep your hips perfectly stable and strong.

This drill is great for developing an awareness of what stable hips feel like, what propelling yourself straight feels like and what running with your glutes feels like. It's one of the best ways I know to develop good running technique.

CHEST

As we've already talked about, "sticking your chest out and running tall," can lead to an over-exaggerated arch in your back which will lock your hips and arms. You'll be spending a lot of energy just getting your legs and arms unstuck, as opposed to letting them swing in a pendulum smoothly.

How you hold your chest and torso is less about what you do, and more about what you don't do.

You don't want to scrunch yourself or lean forward at all. Despite great runners looking like they're leaning forward, actively leaning forward takes a lot of precious energy that we need to conserve. Hunching over is a bad athletic stance that doesn't allow you to move freely.

Instead of sticking your chest out, hunching over or leaning forward, you want to have a neutral, but activated, torso. Try this: stand upright and get someone to push directly down on your shoulders while you resist the force, trying to stay perfectly upright. When you do this, you'll notice some stabilizer muscles activate, the exact muscles that you feel activate will be unique to you.

That feeling of being nice and upright with those stabilizer muscles turned on, that's how you want to feel when running. This position will be a nice, neutral torso that isn't locked out, hunched over or wasting energy leaning forward. You'll be 100% free to let your legs and arms do their jobs.

ARMS

Arms are the most under-utilized body part when it comes to running. In 2019 Challenge Roth when I started getting tired around the 27 km mark, for some reason, the image of USA Olympian Ben Kanute running came to mind. Ben has a distinct arm drive, and like most of us, he wasn't a natural born runner. He had to work hard to get to where he's at.

While my legs wanted to fade and stop moving, I kept pumping my arms hard, which then drove my legs. It got to the point in the run that I felt like I was working my arms harder than I was working my legs. The result was a 3:24 marathon. I didn't walk once, passing hundreds of people in the race.

The arms help balance the body, help drive the legs and provide additional spring to each running stride. If used in the wrong way, they can use a ton of energy and lock up your run so you have to use way more energy with every stride you take.

The difference between good and bad running arm position is small, and even if I provided pictures in this book, it wouldn't communicate the exact spot you want to hold your arms. So, absolutely go to the videos at my website for *Running Foundations* here, mymottiv.com/runfoundations, to see the nuances of arm positioning for the best benefit.

Generally, if you look at the efficient runners in triathlon versus elite track runners, you'll notice their arms are held a little higher, and the shoulders a touch higher, too. The elbows are held a little bit further back instead of pumping out in front like an elite runner, building a little bit of tension in the arms.

This higher elbow position and tiny bit of tension reduces the total movement of the arms saving energy, while also creating an easy snapping effect of the arms without having to forcefully work to drive them.

A quick way to get your arms into the right position is to stand neutrally, then raise the inside of your wrists so they're touching your ribs between your nipples and the bottom of your rib cage. Activate your shoulders slightly so that they raise maybe 1/16", then pull your arms back another 1/16".

You should feel a bit of tension across the front of your body. This will transfer down into a good snap with your leg swing. Now swing your arms like a pendulum with each stride, moving equally forward and backward. When you first start running with this motion, it's a good idea to consciously think about the position for several weeks until it becomes normal.

This position with the arms can be one of the most powerful tools you have on race day that most triathletes aren't thinking of. They're running on tired legs without a backup. You've got a deadly weapon with those arms.

HEAD AND EYES

A lot of run coaches will tell athletes to look out at the horizon when they're running. I think this can open the door to some problems. It's still possible to look at the horizon when you're leaning back, which can cause you to land with your foot in front of your center of mass, slowing you down, potentially causing injuries and just being an inefficient way to run.

I recommend you casually gaze (casual, not a Border Collie locked-in stare) at a spot 50-100 feet in front of you. Pete Jacobs, the 2012 IRONMAN World Champion and holder of one of the fastest runs ever done at IRONMAN Kona, once told me this 50-100-foot spot is a great way to run upright without leaning backwards.

The final technique I want you to think about for triathlon running is relaxing your neck, jaw and lower lip. Even if you get all the other pieces of technique right, you can undo a lot of that progress by being too tense in your neck or face.

Sarah True said once that she thinks about a very relaxed jaw that's so loose, her lower lip almost bounces. By relaxing the neck and jaw, you'll allow all the good points of running technique we've worked on to do their job.

There you have it. Those techniques are the building blocks to allow all the training we've talked about to happen without injury. Get your triathlon running technique right and you'll get faster sooner. You'll also be so much less likely to walk at any point in the run because you'll be efficient, saving as much energy as possible.

Before moving on from technique entirely, I want to spend a little time addressing injuries. The slowest triathlete is an injured one who can't train or race.

Before we move into the next chapter, I need to address injury prevention. I've often referred to running as an injury Cracker Jack box; if you run more, you know you're going to get injured, but you can't predict what that injury will be. It's an unwanted surprise.

This is the double-edged sword of triathlon training. Cycling and running provide the biggest returns on investment to make improvements in your triathlon race times. In the 2019 IRONMAN World Championship, of the top-10 overall finishers in both the men's and women's races, either seven or eight of those top-10 finishers had one of the top-10 bikes or runs, while only three of the top-10 overall athletes had one of the top-10 swims. Looking at that evidence alone, I think it's pretty clear we've got no choice but to focus heavily on our bike and run.

The run can be hard to work on because it's the sport that creates the most injuries when focusing on it more. Personally, I'm very injury prone when it comes to running. I was terrified when I looked at my first training week for Challenge Roth created by Dr. Dan Plews. That plan had six runs in the first week. Astoundingly, though, I didn't have any issues with injuries while training for Challenge Roth that year.

Even though this book gives you a system to run very well with a maximum of three runs a week, we want you to run as much as you want, never having to worry about it. So, in this section, we'll give some guidelines to help you avoid injury as much as possible.

One last thing. If you're starting off new, expect running to feel pretty rough for a couple of months, even if you're running a couple times a week. If you've run before but have taken some time off, you too can expect the first couple weeks to feel rough. Don't worry. Your body will get used to it. Running won't always feel like someone poured quick drying cement into your legs.

PREVENT INJURIES BEFORE THEY HAPPEN

The best way to prevent an injury is to address it before it becomes an injury. Rarely do injuries go from zero to 100, that 100 being a massive injury relegating you to the sideline. Typically, there are warning signs an injury is looming: being overly tired, feeling achy, getting poor sleep, workouts feeling harder than they should, tons of niggles, little aches, pains, and extreme soreness the next day.

Manage the issues I just mentioned and you'll get ahead of injuries before they happen. Here are some guidelines for your overall training that'll reduce the likelihood of an injury popping up:

> ➢ Get more than seven hours of sleep a night (this is a minimum).
> ➢ Only do fasted workouts if they're completely easy
> ➢ Eat within 30 minutes of completing a workout.
> ➢ Have at least two easier days each week. Ideally these days are still workout days but they're easier, which will get the blood flowing and enhance recovery.
> ➢ Have an easier week every third or fourth week.
> ➢ Take your heart rate cap seriously, really, really seriously, and do 70-80% of your total annual training time under this heart rate cap.
> ➢ See a physiotherapist before an injury happens for an assessment of imbalances and weaknesses that you

need to work on. Address these with at least one or two strength/maintenance sessions each week.

Forget about recovery boots, weekly massages, or ice baths. The above points should eliminate the vast majority of all injuries and sicknesses you could experience in triathlon. I'm not saying recovery tools aren't important, but they're the icing on the cake. The basics I listed above are the foundation that all health and fitness is built upon. Get these guidelines wrong and it doesn't matter how much your trigger point ball vibrates, you're still going to develop injuries.

If you've done all the basic things I just listed and you still end runs feeling a little beat up, or you wake up the next day feeling rusty, you would benefit from some of my favourite injury prevention tools that only cost a few dollars.

Get yourself a tennis ball, a spiked trigger point ball and a foam roller. With just these three things, you can work out all of the knots and overlapped or stiff muscles that might be causing discomfort and could potentially lead to injury.

With all these injury prevention tools, you should use them to put as much pressure as you can handle on the area that hurts, roll back and forth and around that painful area, until the pain either releases or goes away by at least 50%. You might have to do this every day for five to 10 minutes while watching TV, but that five to 10 minutes could very well keep you running for a lifetime.

Finally, there are a couple of ways you should use your running shoes to reduce the likelihood of injury. First, try to keep your shoes new to keep the foam from collapsing. Second, cycle shoes in-and-out so you're never running on the same pair on back-to-back days. Shoe foam takes as much as 48 hours to recover from a run.

I'll talk more about shoe selection and care in a later section dedicated strictly to shoes. But to summarize, with regard to injury prevention, your shoes should be new and fresh.

HOW TO PREVENT INJURIES FROM GETTING WORSE

Even if you've followed all of these guidelines, you might still get injured from running. Taking 10,000-20,000 hard steps on pavement is damaging to the body. Injuries are bound to pop up.

But when does a niggle or ache turn into something worth looking into? I adhere to these three rules to determine when it's time to bring in the professionals:

1. In the following two to three days after a run, a specific pain doesn't go away.
2. After 15 minutes of warming up for a run, pain doesn't go away.

3. If I've been dealing with the same pain for three weeks or more.

In each of these cases, it's time to go see a physiotherapist. I recommend a physiotherapist over a specialist (say a podiatrist for a foot injury) because a physiotherapist will assess the area, and the body function that might be causing that injury.

For example, when I was dealing with an Achilles injury after the 2017 season, a highly-recommended podiatrist treated me for several months and eventually said, "All of the structures in your foot are fine. You should be OK." But I was still in pain. I went to a physiotherapist who watched slow motion video of me running and saw a weakness in my left glute that was causing my Achilles to shake with each step. He prescribed glute strengthening exercises and my Achilles pain went away.

Start with an endurance sports specific physiotherapist, then see a specialist if they feel it would be a good idea to further improve the function of an area.

DEALING WITH INJURIES WHEN THEY HAPPEN

When you encounter a running injury, BACK OFF! Running injuries can become so severe that if you don't address them quickly, giving your body time to heal, you may never come back to triathlon. Aggravate an injury enough and it can become a permanent problem.

The first thing to do is to respect the recommendations of your physiotherapist and other care providers helping you through the injury. Maybe even be a little extra cautious than their recommendations allow.

When you're dealing with a running injury, that's a good time to focus on additional swims, which might not make you faster instantly but if you can finish the swim portion of a race in the same amount of time but feeling fresher, that will make you faster in the rest of the race, guaranteed.

This is also a good time to focus on becoming a beast on the bike. It was during my heavily injured years that I made some of my biggest gains in triathlon because I was able to make such big gains on the bike; the bike is such a huge portion of the race, I got a lot faster overall.

While dealing with an injury and not being able to run at all, deep water running can provide a similar fitness benefit. There are studies that have shown people making the same running gains from water running as they did from traditional running. I like the Fluid Running deep water running method. I found it to be the best for getting the heart rate up, it doesn't cost much to set up, and the guided workouts make the time go by more quickly.

When you get back into regular running, try to stay on soft surfaces (like packed trails) as they'll be the easiest on your body. Stick to shorter, more frequent runs as opposed to longer ones where you run tired. Running while fatigued is likely to cause an injury—so run fresh and only fresh.

Finally, don't stress too much about injury. Pro triathlete Tim O'Donnell broke his foot and told me that before the 2019 IRONMAN World Championship where he finished second, his longest run on pavement had been just seven miles. Yet, he had the best run of his career in Kona and the best finish he'd ever done. It goes to show that constant huge volumes of running aren't always needed to perform well.

COMMON RUNNING INJURIES AND HOW TO DEAL WITH THEM

I'm not a doctor, I just play one on the internet. Seriously though, consult your doctor about any injury you have. I have had quite a number of running related injuries, so I have a small amount of knowledge about common running injuries and techniques I've personally used to prevent and fix them.

Shin splints: A sharp pain in the front of the shin that can be described as a feeling like a knife is in the front of your lower leg, or that your shin bone is cracking in half. It hurts!

Maybe try: Calf stretching of all sorts helps to alleviate shin splints. One of the best ways I found to prepare your calves for running is to get a stretchy band (a TheraBand, for example) and tie it around a stationary object, then loop the other end around your toes. Pull the band toward you, which helps strengthen the front of your lower leg.

Outer knee pain: A sharp pain on the lower outside of the knee is a common symptom of IT band issues. The IT band runs from the glutei down the side of the upper leg and inserts into the lower outside of the knee, often the exact spot where the pain comes from.

Maybe try: Foam rolling the glutes and outside of your upper leg often fixes this problem fairly quickly.

Lower back pain: Sharp pain in the lower back can be caused by a huge number of things. Spending a lot of time folded at 90 degrees into the seated cycling position tightens our hips and weakens our glutes, which often results in lower back pain day to day, or when running.

Maybe try: One of the absolute best resources I can recommend to fix back pain is called Foundation Training. The very first day our team was in Kona to cover the 2018 IRONMAN World Championship, my back went out as I got out of bed. The back pain was so bad that I had to get my videographer, Melyssa, and my wife, Kim, to carry all of our cumbersome camera gear around the island for the entire week. That back pain was still bad after seeing a massage therapist, physio and two different chiropractors when I got home.

Eventually, Erin Carson, the strength trainer we have produced a number of videos with, turned me onto Foundation

Training which fixed my back problem in literally a few days (no kidding) and it hasn't come back since.

Achilles Tightness: Pain in the Achilles (at the back of the ankle) is one of the most common irritations heavy runners experience.

Maybe try: Eccentric heel drops are the common fix for Achilles pain, but there are a couple little known nuances you should be aware of.

If the pain is directly at the base of the heel, or within an inch of the base of the heel, do the eccentric heel drops on a floor so your heel doesn't dip below the rest of your foot. If your pain is in the belly of the Achilles, an inch or more from the base of the heel, perform the eccentric heel drops on a stair and let the Achilles stretch as the heel dips below the rest of the foot.

Also, the Achilles pain could be coming from tightness in the calf or all the way up the back of the leg. Every single night while watching TV, I'll use a strap or stretchy band to stretch the back of my leg with a two-to-three-minute static stretch. This has been the number one thing I've found to reduce any Achilles issues I've had.

Foot pain: Our feet take a beating when we run, so it's natural to experience some foot pain after a run and in the days following.

Maybe try: I recommend spending some time smashing your foot down onto a spiky trigger point ball after a run. This will release a lot of the tight muscles, so you're less likely to be walking around on beat-up feet. This is more important than you think. If you walk around on beat-up feet, you'll be altering your walking style, potentially leading to a higher likelihood of injury.

Also, this has been a favourite of mine ever since I had to wear suits for a living in my former life as a financial advisor: spend as much time as possible throughout the day barefoot. This will strengthen your feet and make them less likely to get injured.

Plantar Fasciitis: Plantar Fasciitis is a sharp pain at the heel or all the way under the foot; it tends to be worse, right after waking up in the morning and getting out of bed.

Plantar fasciitis is worse at waking because it's often caused by tight calf muscles. When we sleep, our feet tend to plantar-flex (point down) which shortens the calf, making it tight when we wake up.

Maybe try: Plantar Fasciitis is a bit of a tough fix, but I've had the best success with calf and hamstring stretching several times a day, holding at least one of those stretches for at least two minutes.

Take injuries, niggles and little bits of pain seriously. What starts out as a bit of achiness or soreness can quickly turn into a full-blown injury or an overtraining issue. Keep yourself feeling challenged, but overall fresh and not constantly beat down. Address small pains before they become big problems and you'll be able to stay consistent in your training, which is the key to being a better athlete than you ever thought possible.

CHAPTER 4

TRIATHLON RUNNING SETUP

I once spent a week in Tucson, Arizona with two-time USA Olympian in triathlon, Sarah True, and her husband, Ben True. (Ben is also an amazing runner who held the all-time US 5K road record at 13:22. Crazy, right?)

You might think these two athletes, some of the best runners in the world, have their running gear dialled in to the exact, best possible setup. Specifically chosen shoes, the best running watch possible (with a screen customized to have the optimal fields showing), brand new heart rate monitors… But you'd be wrong if that's what you pictured.

Ben is sponsored by Garmin. He told me Garmin always asks him what he wants in a running watch. "If it can tell me the time of day, I'm pretty happy," he said.

You might think Ben's an outlier. But, when Sarah was talking about her shoe selection, she said, "I really love these new HOKAs they sent me, they feel great!" I asked her which model they were and she said, "Good question. I don't know." She didn't look at the model, the heel-to-toe drop, how much the shoe weighed or how much carbon was in the shoe. HOKA sent out boxes of shoes for her to try and she used what felt right.

I'll go one step farther to reinforce that Sarah and Ben aren't just luddites. I once got paced for a 5000 meter time trial track run by Corey Gallagher, who was the reigning World Beer Mile Champion, and winner of just about every major local running race over the previous few years. He asked me what I thought I would be able to run. I told him a 19:30, which works out to 93.6 seconds for every 400-meter lap.

Corey nodded and said, "Got it!" But I looked at his wrist and saw he wasn't wearing a watch. I walked over to the friend who had arranged the time trial and asked how Corey was going to pace me. He said, "He'll just dial in the pace." Apparently, he knew exactly what every pace felt like.

During the first lap of the run, I was constantly looking at the laptop on my wrist (aka, my running watch) to make sure Corey wasn't way off the pace and was going to blow me up. As we passed the lap marker, the person timing the run yelled out, "95 seconds!" Corey was within one-and-a-half seconds of the target. The next lap was, "92 seconds." After that, he dialled it right in, and every single lap was either "93 seconds," or "94 seconds" like clockwork.

Corey let me go on my own for the final two laps. I did the time trial in 19:22. I was amazed at how metronome-like he was with his pacing, even though that pace was totally foreign to him. It was almost a minute slower per kilometer than his normal race effort.

I went over to my buddy and (after nearly throwing up from the effort of the run), I asked how Corey did that. Was he was just known for being a savant with paces? My buddy said, "No, that's what good runners can do. All these gadgets, and watches and tech, that's so amateur. Every good runner can tell you their pace within a few seconds by feel."

I get a lot of messages from triathletes asking which watch I use, what shoes they should get, do I run with a power meter. Occasionally, they say they're holding back on running much because they're waiting until they get the right gear. First off, get out and train no matter how limited your gear is. Secondly, rarely do I respond because my answer always is, "It doesn't matter, do whatever you can afford and feels comfortable." That obviously shocks the heck out of people, given that I'm on YouTube and Instagram, reviewing $400 Nike shoes, and taking pictures of my workout details on a high-end Garmin watch.

My gear closest wasn't always so full. For my first six years in triathlon, I ran only with a heart rate monitor, even though I didn't know how to use heart rate to train. I used the watch to see how fast my pace was after the run. I also wore shoes so long that the lugs on the front of most of my Newton runners wore down to literally nothing. And you know what? It was during this time that I made my biggest run performance gains.

The reason I review all different kinds of shoes, watches and tracking devices on YouTube isn't because I obsess over them as a crucial tool for my own training. I do that because everyone else obsesses over them as "crucial" tools for training. The videos get a lot of views, so I make them because they obviously help people in some way.

This isn't to say you should forget about every last bit of nice running gear you own and run in Chuck Taylor Converse shoes and cotton Fruit of the Loom t-shirts. By all means, get the high-end shoes, sweat-wicking shirts, heart rate monitors, power meters and all of the other running gear available to you. It can certainly be a benefit. But *IT IS NOT CRUCIAL TO SUCCESSFUL RUN TRAINING!*

In this section, I'm going to briefly discuss a lot of the common pieces of running gear that athletes either need to buy, such as shoes, or consider buying, such as heart rate monitors and power meters.

I'll explain how I recommend purchase decisions should be made, and how to use these tools in training. When it comes right down to it, don't ever let any purchase decision of running gear hold you back from what's paramount to your run training: running.

RUNNING SHOES

There's a Mexican tribe deep in the hills of the Copper Canyon in Sierra Madre called the Tarahumara. This tribe is known for their incredible endurance, running multiple marathons a day to trade or communicate with others. They do this wearing minimal sandals made of old car tires (or they even go barefoot). The tribe is free from many diseases and war, and the tribe members appear happy and healthy.

In 2009, the Tarahumara entered the main stream when the book, *Born to Run*, was published, creating an explosion of runners and triathletes who started running in extremely minimal shoes, or even running barefoot. While *Born to Run* is one of my all-time favourite books because it got me thinking more independently, the rapid increase in people using minimal running shoes has kept podiatrist waiting rooms full, and orthopedic surgeon waitlists long—all due to massive spikes in foot injuries.

People are certainly meant to be barefoot more often than we currently are in the modern world: around the house, in the backyard, even running lightly in grass is great for overall foot strength and thus foot health. But humans aren't designed to run on artificially hard surfaces like asphalt and concrete.

Running on these surfaces is tremendously hard on the body and requires cushioned shoes. Of course, there are obvious exceptions of people in less modern societies who've been barefoot most of their lives, running in almost minimal shoes. In the West, however, we spend most of our lives in cushioned shoes. Our feet will never be as strong as someone who has spent a lifetime barefoot. Now, there are certainly some people who gravitated toward barefoot-style running, totally reducing their injuries and will never go back to shoes. But they're the exception.

Think about running tracks, where you're running hard and the force on your body is at its max. Do this on a basic asphalt running track, and you'll feel incredibly beat up from the workout. If that track is a softer surface, you'll probably feel fast during the workout and fresh afterward.

I believe, and the evidence supports this, that despite what the barefoot marathon runners would have you think, you need to wear cushioned shoes. However, going too cushioned, too structured and getting too many features could be just as big a problem as trying to run a half-marathon with bare little piggies.

The first pair of running shoes I owned were flimsy Payless runners. But at least they got me "running" (well, it was more like shuffling when I first started out). When I decided to upgrade to some proper runners, I went to the local big box running shoe store and asked them to recommend the best pair for me. They had me walk back and forth in the store barefoot, concluding I was an over-pronator. That meant I needed structured shoes to stabilize my foot. Because I was new to running, I also needed a big built-up heel to cushion my landing. I assumed they were the experts, so I got the shoes they suggested. I then subsequently spent the next two years battling shin splints, painful knees and a sore lower back.

Fortunately, I ended up reading *Born to Run.* While the barefoot idea was a little extreme for me, I started thinking that maybe I should consider different running shoes. I called up a friend who had been a university track runner, and who worked his way through school at a small local running store. I asked him what shoes resulted in the fewest injuries and best running for his customers (because it was a local store so heavily involved in the running community, he knew how his customers were doing.)

He told me the running shoe industry propaganda about stability shoes, structured shoes, over-pronating and under-pronating shoes is all hype. Let's say you're an over-pronator and you get shoes to correct that. Your foot still over-pronates when you run. It just does it in a different shoe. That shoe, in a way, "protects" the over-pronation, so your body never has to deal with (and thus strengthen your body to handle) the over-pronation which is always going to happen. Instead, the super fancy stability shoes allow the body to stay weak and almost ensure you'll eventually get injured. He said that for almost all people, a neutral shoe, paired with a very slow increase in running mileage so you can adapt to running, is the best way to go.

Big, built-up heels with a big heel-to-toe drop to cushion your landing creates similar problems for new runners because it prevents your body from running in its natural movement pattern.

In *Running Rewired,* a book by Jay Dicharry, he talks about many cases where talented high school runners with odd running techniques would get to college where their new "sophisticated" run coach would change their running form to a more traditional method. Dicharry cites that, time after time, he's had to piece these athletes back together after a series of injuries caused by that new running form.

Dicharry explains that everyone has a unique movement pattern and body structure. Trying to shoehorn your movement pattern into a drastically different one will likely cause injury because it's forcing your body to do something unnatural.

Using shoes with built-up heels is one form of forcing your body into an unnatural running form because your body is designed to walk around without your heel being higher than the ball of your foot. The best running shoe for new runners is one with minimal heel-to-toe drop. Again, the studies support this.

One study looked at running injury rates, comparing shoes with built-up heels versus minimal heel-to-toe drop shoes, and it compared these in both new and seasoned runners. The study suggested that for new runners, the minimal heel-to-toe drop shoes created fewer injuries than built-up heel shoes. The shoe allowed the body to move naturally. But in the seasoned runners, the minimal heel-to-toe drop shoes created slightly more injuries.[5]

I know some of you might be saying, "Listen, Taren, my podiatrist said I had to wear orthotics/heel lifts/structured shoes." Yeah, so did mine. Until it got me more injured.

During the winter of 2017-18, as I alluded to earlier in this book, I was dealing with an Achilles injury caused by overtraining and too much running at moderate intensities. I went to a podiatrist who said, "Taren, your Achilles is injured so we've got to take all the stress off of it that we can. Go get some 10-millimeter heel lifts with big arch support for all your runners." I gave him the benefit of the doubt and did what he said. As I started running again, my Achilles just got worse.

I was frustrated and needed help. I went to a physiotherapist specializing in treating runners. I told him what I was doing with

---

[5] https://www.ncbi.nlm.nih.gov/pubmed/27501833

my shoes, even bringing them with me to the appointment along with some slow-motion running footage of myself. He looked at the footage and noticed my left knee was collapsing inward every time my left foot landed. He tested my glutei and sure enough, my left glutes were so inactive that they weren't strong enough to stabilize my left leg when I was running, and the shake of the left leg was likely aggravating my Achilles.

He also told me to take the lifts out of my shoes and spend more time barefoot around the house. My foot needed to strengthen and my Achilles would have to learn to stabilize itself. He said the arch support and heel lifts take so much pressure off the foot that I might have some short-term relief, but using those items doesn't force the lower leg structure to deal with anything, allowing the lower leg to atrophy. He said, "What happens when the lower leg isn't strong enough to deal with new arch support and heel lifts anymore? You're going to have to get more arch support and a bigger heel lift over and over until eventually you can't function because you'll be running in high heels."

I went back to my neutral shoes without heel lifts or arch support and started doing a series of glute-strengthening exercises. Magically, within a few weeks, I was running pain free. I haven't had that Achilles problem return, even though in 2019 I did the biggest running volume I've ever done in a year by a long shot.

Of course, as I've said, I'm not a doctor. Always, always, always check with a medical professional before making any changes. I recommend finding a physiotherapist specializing in caring for elite runners. They've dealt with more run-specific injuries than anyone. They're focused on fixing the root cause of a problem and less on Band-Aid solutions.

Here's a fast recap of those guidelines for shoe selection:

> ➢ Unless instructed otherwise by a run-specific medical professional, select neutral running shoes.
> ➢ Runners in their first two to three years of running should select shoes with heel-to-toe drops of 0-6 millimeters to build up musculoskeletal strength to support their natural movement pattern.
> ➢ If you've learned to run over a number of years in natural, low heel-to-toe drop shoes and have avoided injury, you can start trying shoes with a slightly larger heel-to-toe drop if they feel natural when you run.
> ➢ Look for shoes with a moderate weight that aren't so light they don't provide any cushion, but aren't so heavy that they're hard to swing back and forth. Personally, 7-10 ounces seems to be the sweet spot, with the lighter shoes in the range being great for racing and the heavier shoes better for training.

Finally, I need to address how often you should change your running shoes. Unfortunately, the answer is probably more often than you might think. Running in old runners is one of the number-one ways to get injured. You've got to keep those kicks fresh!

Running shoes last anywhere from 100-400 miles before the foam brakes down. The shoes won't provide any cushion or energy return after that. The amount of time your shoes will last depends on several factors. Super-fast Nike Vaporfly runners only last about 100 miles because the foam, while incredibly good for energy return, breaks down easily.

Generally, the lighter the shoe and the less rubber it has on the sole, the shorter it will last, typically needing to be replaced within 200 miles. If you're not a natural runner, or you're a bigger athlete, your shoes won't last as long. You'll create more impact on the shoe, breaking it down quicker. The heavier shoes (often called "daily trainers") with rubber on the sole will often last longer, withstanding upward of 200-400 miles.

I tend to replace shoes frequently, always erring on the side of running in shoes for fewer miles before changing over to a new pair. Even if I have to spend an extra $200-300 a year for newer shoes more often, that's still cheaper than having to spend money on physiotherapy to fix running injuries because of old shoes.

Also, I rotate shoes throughout the week because the foam in running shoes takes anywhere from 24-48 hours to completely recover between runs. I'll use light and fast shoes like a HOKA One Carbon X or a Nike Vaporfly for my super-fast runs, a more moderate shoe like a HOKA Rincon for my shorter brick runs and something more beefy like a HOKA Bondi or a Nike Zoom Fly for the longer, slower runs.

The best piece of advice I can give regarding running shoes is this: if your feet, ankles or lower legs are sore after a number of runs and it's been a little while since you changed shoes, it's time for a new pair. Lower leg pain is the first sign that your shoes are too old and need to be replaced. Listen to your body more than you listen to the guidelines of how long running shoes "should" last.

HEART RATE MONITORING DEVICE

This is the only piece of tech I'm going to say is a must have for running. Everything else is entirely optional. Notice that I didn't include the words "running watch" in the title for this section? That's because you don't need one. You can get great training with as little as a heart rate monitor strap paired to your smartphone.

The reason I consider monitoring your heart rate during training a critical behavior, is because running is hard on the body. As we discussed in the long run section, using heart rate paired with the Zone Training, you can customize for yourself with the calculators at mymottiv.com/runfoundations. You should stay injury free, making progress for years.

I'm not partial to any one specific heart rate monitor. Personally, I used the Wahoo chest strap because it's accurate and reliable. It also pairs to phones easily and has a good training app, but other chest straps are good too. Arm straps are slightly less accurate than chest straps, but they're a good option if chest straps chafe you. I wouldn't recommend wrist heart rate monitors. In my experience, and from what I've heard from other reviewers online, they can be off by as many as 20-30 beats per minute.

If you want to geek out over tech, I highly recommend the DC Rainmaker website. It's packed with comprehensive reviews on everything from heart rate monitors to action cameras and smart bike trainer software. When I'm looking for sports tech, I look to his site first.

The main place you'll want to use the heart rate monitor is during your long run, where you'll set a cap based on the calculation you'll do in the spreadsheet available here, at mymottiv.com/runfoundations. You'll do most of your running under that heart rate cap.

For the weekly intense run, I recommend using rate of perceived exertion instead of heart rate, because heart rate lags. It's possible for you to do a 30-second hard running interval and not even hit your max heart rate during the interval; the max heart rate could peak well after you've finished the 30 seconds because heart rate lags that much. That's why I recommend using rate of perceived exertion for the fast stuff.

Get yourself a heart rate monitor and learn to love it!

That's it. Just a good pair of running shoes and an accurate heart rate monitor. The only two things I'd classify as must-have items. Everything beyond this is a total luxury. And frankly, even if you don't have a great pair of shoes or a heart rate monitor, you shouldn't let that stop you. You just have to be a little more careful to hold yourself back with running mileage and pace to make sure you don't get injured.

In the next section, I'll dive into the multitude of gear and gadgets that I'm sure will be a lot more interesting to you. My thoughts on running power meters, shorts, singlets, sunglasses, running watches and all the other odds and ends you could consider getting (or should skip and save your money.)

This is the list of running gear that, if it doesn't stress you out to spend money on, great! If you don't have any of these items, great, still get out and run. No big deal. Call these the *nice to haves* but not *need to haves*.

The items I'm highlighting are strictly the running gear items that both a) fit into the running workouts we discuss here and b) serve a function specifically for triathletes. We could explore trail running, marathon training, hiking or whatever rabbit hole you want and make this section 100 pages long. Instead, we're only going to address the items that'll likely serve you in some fashion with the training we've discussed here and also prescribe on our MōTTIV training app.

We're also only going to shed light on the *should I*, or *shouldn't I buy this* questions. We'll ignore the basics and items that would be personal to you, like hats or earbuds.

Finally, I'll also list these in order of what I feel is the best return on your dollars from the smartest purchase to the least critical. This list could get long, so let's dive right in.

MUSIC/PODCASTS

Running purists are going to hate me for this because old school runners and track athletes say that running with music or podcasts is a crutch that'll make you mentally weak and hurt your run performance. You know what else will hurt your run performance? Not running enough because it's more boring than a conversation with a bowl of oatmeal.

Most age group triathletes I talk to say running is boring. This is why we break the workouts on the MōTTIV training app into chunks, giving our athletes more manageable pieces, thus helping with the mental aspect of running. It's also why I say that if you want to run with music or podcasts, go for it!

Studies [6] confirm that music during workouts enhances athletic performance and enjoyment of exercise. So, even if you can't use music in a race, it's likely that you'll perform better in races if you had trained with music, because your training will be more frequent and you'll be able to push harder or longer.

We amateur triathletes don't need that extra 0.5% mental edge gained by training and racing the exact same way and developing mental toughness. We need regularity. Anything promoting consistency and regularity is cool with me. Of course, if you like the calming aspect of running without music or podcasts, then stick with that.

Don't fuss about what you use to get audio in your ears. Earbuds, headphones, corded earbuds, a speaker on the bike of someone riding alongside you. I've used them all. They're all fine.

ELASTIC LACES

Elastic laces aren't a must-have because you can definitely tie up your shoes without them, but they're one of the quickest and cheapest ways to get faster in your races.

It's likely when you get off the bike in your races, your hands won't be as nimble as normal. The bike portion a race can be

---

[6] https://www.ncbi.nlm.nih.gov/pubmed/25202850

cool. You might be gripping the handlebars extra tight. There's a lot of blood in your legs and arms and less in your delicate fingers. There's plenty of excitement going on in transition, so it's normal to have shoe-tying amnesia in T2.

I've seen hundreds of people stuck in transition, losing minutes trying to get their shoes on. I've witnessed people having to stop mid-run to tie their shoes. Fun fact: I ran the entire 21.1 km of the half marathon at IM 70.3 Puerto Rico with one shoe undone because I didn't double-knot it. I probably had 50 people yell out, "Hey Taren, your shoe's undone!" I knew it... and I felt silly.

Elastic laces are a no brainer for Sprint and Olympic distance triathlons where seconds matter a lot. One of the downsides to elastic laces, however, is that they often scrunch up a shoe, so they can cause a small amount of chaffing or even create a blister. For this reason, I say elastic laces are optional for 70.3 and IRONMAN distance events where comfort over a long run is more important than gaining a few seconds in transition.

RUNNING WATCH

This is what everyone was waiting for. "What watch do you use?" is the single most asked question I get on social media. I almost never answer it because it literally does not matter. For the record, as of writing this I use the Garmin... *ummmm...*

something. I actually don't know the model. 935XT? Yes, I seriously just double-checked the model of my watch while typing this paragraph because that's how little the watch matters.

This isn't to say training watches aren't useful tools. I feel that monitoring heart rate during long runs is a critical aspect of success in triathlon training. While you can monitor your heart rate with a smartphone hooked up to a heart rate monitor, it's not ideal. It's bulky and the screens go to sleep after a few minutes. Having a running watch makes it easy to get your heart rate in a second with just a glance.

Here's how I use a running watch during racing and training. I set up the screen with heart rate, lap pace, total time and average pace (which I only use during races). I then set the lap notification to go off every kilometer. This allows me to glance at the watch frequently at the start of a run, cross-reference that with what the lap pace is, and it starts dialing me into a pace "feeling" that I'll be able to run that day. After 10 to 15 minutes, I barely have to look at my watch. I give it a glance every time the lap notification goes off to make sure my heart rate is under my heart rate cap, and adjust my pace accordingly.

Having pace data for runs is helpful for building confidence in your training. As you use the heart rate cap more often, you'll find your pace gets faster at the same heart rate. I use the pace feature to build confidence, not to guide the pace.

The only time I use a running watch during the intense run is to mark my splits. If I'm doing a series of 400-meter intervals on the track, I'll time the first few and use that as a benchmark for what I have to hit for the rest of the workout. If I'm doing longer intervals of four to eight minutes, I'll use the workout total time to set my start and end points, and use the lap button to mark the start and stop.

These functions are pretty basic. Based on what I hear from a lot of the best pros in the world, this is more than they'll even use. They're so tuned into their bodies, they don't fuss about the details. I'd encourage you to not rely on the data too much during your runs. Don't become reliant on the watch to tell you what to do. Instead, build a sense for how different paces feel and what's sustainable without looking at a watch. This is a powerful tool when you get into a race because you'll be able to dial your race effort up or down to the exact fastest pace you can manage depending on how your body is feeling that day.

I recommend whatever watch you can afford. All watches are pretty good these days for the basic functions listed above. Don't feel like you need to get a watch that works in the pool because the pool clock is a better training tool. Don't feel like you need to get a watch that has multiple triathlon functions because some of the best races are done strictly by feel. And don't feel like you need to get a watch with ton of cadence, stride length, vertical oscillation, yada, yada, yada features.

Use the DC Rainmaker website to read up on the watches within your budget, and get whichever one you like the sound of. Don't be a slave to a laptop on your wrist.

RECOVERY SHOES

Seeing recovery shoes so high up on the list of running gear to consider might surprise you, because a lot of people don't know what recovery shoes are yet. They're a bit of a new marketing term for an old type of shoe.

These are squishy, cushy shoes that are comfortable to walk in. They take a little bit of the load off your joints and muscles. I love them.

After IM 70.3 Atlantic City in 2019, I was really stiff during the couple of days after the race. So stiff that, the day after the race, I woke up and immediately booked a massage so I could hopefully function as I packed up and flew home. Fortunately, I had purchased a brand-new pair of Oofos before the race. While I didn't intend on being *that guy* walking around airports in my lounging shoes, I decided to wear them on my travel day.

Normally, travel days after a race really beat up my body. All the sore muscles and joints stiffen up. I have to spend the next couple days at home getting rid of that rigidity and soreness. Instead, after I got home from IM 70.3 AC, the time I spent walking around the airport in my new Oofos had loosened up my muscles. It was one of the quickest races recoveries I ever had.

Anything promoting faster recovery is high on my cool gear list. Recovery shoes like the ones by Oofos, HOKA, or even Crocs, are the ones I'd lean toward.

RUNNING SPECIFIC SOCKS

You might see me, Lucy Charles-Barclay or Laura Philipp rocking the bright and fun, high-end Sporcks running and cycling socks on Instagram. I love them! They're flashy, they've got a little bit of compression but not so much that they alter the natural foot shape, and they're nice and high so they show off the bright design. Does that mean you have to get them? Nope.

That said, I don't recommend running in basic white athletic socks. They have too much material. They can bunch and fold in your shoes, causing blisters. They're also either too heavy not allowing the foot to breathe, or flimsy and will fall apart with a small amount of training.

Running socks should fit snugly, but not tight (I'll talk about tight compression socks in a bit). They need to be light enough for your foot to breathe so the sock doesn't become damp (which causes blisters), while remaining tough enough to not develop holes (which will also cause blisters.)

Most running socks at a running store will be fine. The differences between a five-dollar pair of socks and a thirty-dollar pair isn't huge. There's also no difference (that I know about) between a low-cut sockette and the high socks I wear today. Frankly, IRONMAN World Champion Jan Frodeno started wearing the high socks when he won his first IRONMAN World Championship and the world has been all high socks all the time ever since.

Should you go with or without socks in races? For Sprint and Olympic triathlons, I recommend no socks because seconds matter in those shorter races. Leading into the race, you'll want to start doing at least one short weekly run without socks to toughen your feet up (the weekly brick run is perfect for this.) When you're setting up your transition area, you'll also benefit from putting a bunch of baby powder in your running shoes so your foot stays dry during the run. Also, smear Vaseline all around every area of the shoe edges and inside the tongue so you have less likelihood of developing a blister.

It's much less critical to save time in transition in half-IRONMAN and IRONMAN races by going barefoot. If you're going for an age group title, or trying to qualify for a world championship, you might want to consider going sockless. But even Jan Frodeno and Daniela Ryf wore running socks in the 2019 IM 70.3 World Championship, and those were some of the fastest 70.3 races ever performed. For full Iron-distance events, wear socks.

Finally, when you choose to wear socks in a race, also squirt some baby powder in the socks so your foot and your shoe are extra, extra dry. Don't worry about Vaseline in your shoe if you're wearing socks.

ARM SLEEVES

Arm sleeves are covers that fit tightly over your arms from the wrist up to just under the arm pit. They serve to either keep you warm, or keep the sun off your skin, keeping you cool.

Living in Canada, where it's very cold during parts of the year, I use arm sleeves when the temperature dips under 12 degrees Celsius (54 Fahrenheit). Also, because I live in Canada, I often don't get a savage tan. When I go to hot weather races, my skin can crisp up and burn quickly, which hurts performance. I've used the same uninsulated arm sleeves in both cold weather and hot, sunny days.

Whether you're racing a cold race or a hot one, I highly recommend arm sleeves. For cold weather races, put the sleeves on before the swim under your wetsuit. For hot races that aren't done in a wetsuit, put the sleeves on in Transition 1.

Don't underestimate the toll heat and cold place on your body in a race or in training. Thermogenesis is the system of body functions that heat your body when it's cold, and cool your body when it's hot. It takes a huge amount of energy to perform these tasks. Help your body out by doing whatever you can to regulate your body temperature.

RUNNING POWER METER

A running power meter is a foot pod that provides a measurement, in watts, of how much power you're putting out while running. High-end running foot pod power meters also allow you to do interactive running, like on Zwift.

The training and racing benefit to running power meters is that they give a more standardized metric to use when pace ends up becoming almost irrelevant, like when running on hills or in windy conditions.

With high-end running foot pods, like the Stryd power meter, when you run up a hill or into the wind, you get a power reading that tells you how many watts you're putting out so you can moderate your effort. This allows you to make sure you're pacing yourself evenly, even though your pace and heart rate might be drastically different than on flat land.

Stryd power meters and the like also provide metrics like ground contact time, leg stiffness and running cadence. You can analyze your training to see what kind of run workouts you need to do to become more well-rounded. With myself, for instance, I saw that while my top end speed was good, during a 70.3 half-marathon, my leg stiffness would break down around the 13 km mark. I needed to build up my muscle durability by simply running more often.

Power meters can certainly be beneficial, but they're not a game changer in my opinion. I tend to look at gear from an 95/5 standpoint. The basic five percent of the things you do (see: training frequency, proper training, recovery, nutrition) will cover 95% of your results. The 95% of the gear you could obsess about will only contribute to five percent of the results. I would put running power meters in the "Only contribute to the final five percent of results" category. However, if you love data and money's not a concern, or want to run on Zwift, go for a running foot pod.

NOTE: The Zwift run pod is only able to communicate with Zwift running and doesn't feature all the extra data points I mentioned. The Stryd is currently the leading running power meter and can be used both in Zwift running and in regular training.

FUEL BELT

A fuel belt is a waist belt you wear while running to carry your nutrition, hydration, etc. I have a love/hate relationship with fuel belts because a lot of people use them incorrectly.

Look at the run groups of any local running store and you'll see so many runners carrying a fuel belt with several bottles of fluids and some gels. My issue with this usage is that most of these groups go for 45 to 60 minute runs. Nutrition isn't necessary at those distances and it results in athletes becoming dependent on sugar to get them through even short amounts of exercise. They're likely to bonk in their races.

While all the nuances of nutrition will be discussed in our book, *Triathlon Nutrition Foundations,* you don't need to consume calories for any workout shorter than 75 minutes. When you become fit and nutritionally sound, you can even get through two to three hours of low intensity training without calories (though you should still take on fluids).

I recommend athletes use fuel belts primarily for hydration. If you follow the nutrition guidelines outlined in *Triathlon Nutrition Foundations,* you'll be able to even do your long two- to three-hour IRONMAN training runs without calories, and you'll become bonk-proof in your races. If you're new to triathlon, bring calories for runs longer than 75 minutes. But to reiterate: you shouldn't be taking on calories for any run shorter than 75 minutes.

CHAFE BUTTER/NIPPLE COVERS/TOE PROTECTORS

I have to address the issue of keeping all our tender bits safe. Most people don't talk about it, but chaffing is real. Chaffing from wetsuits tends to be more common than chaffing from running, but people still often get bloody nipples from their running shirts, rubbing on the arm pits or blisters on the toes from their shoes and socks.

Personally, I'm not a fan of using the various options to prevent rubbing. They don't allow the skin to toughen-up and create a resiliency against what inevitably will happen. In the first few years of running, because I wasn't running a ton, I got a lot of blisters on my toes in races. I tried everything from Band-Aids to gel toe covers to something called an invisible Band-Aid, but I kept getting blisters. No matter how much I covered up, my feet were always so delicate, any tiny spot I missed would blister badly.

Eventually, I stopped using anything. I ran more frequently each week, but for shorter intervals—and only in a training setting—so my feet weren't wet like in a race. My feet toughened up, and eventually I didn't need anything to prevent blisters. I could even go from running in socks to immediately running sockless without much worry about a blister.

If you're chaffing, instead of totally trying to prevent it, I recommend embracing the chafe... a little. For longer runs, certainly use a small amount of anti-chafe cream, but avoid the covers; the cream will take the edge off the chaffing. Then, for all of your shorter runs, use nothing and eventually your skin will toughen up so chaffing won't be an issue anymore. Also, if you've got a decent pair of socks and good fitting shoes, it'll reduce your foot blister problems.

RACE BELT

This is the elastic belt that goes around your waist holding your bib number in place. It doesn't make you any faster at all. It's a nicer option than safety pinning your bib number to your race kit. This is an entirely optional purchase. Also, if you race often, you'll eventually end up competing in a race where you're given a race belt in your athlete bag at check-in (however, race belts cost less than $10, so you probably don't need to wait to get a race-bag freebie).

There are a couple of benefits to the race belt over safety pins, but they're more a matter of comfort than they are of performance:

Race belts can be put on in transition quickly so you don't have to crumple the paper bib number under a wetsuit or swim skin, potentially ruining them

Race belts can be turned around to the back or the front so they can be seen easily on the bike and the run, respectively

Some higher-end race belts can even hold a little bit of nutrition, like a gel or salt tabs

But, as I said earlier, race belts don't offer much of a performance advantage. You'll look a little more like you fit in, which tends to make most people more confident. If you feel more confident, you'll race more confidently.

Pro tip: many pros tend to wear their race belts not on their waists, but lower on their butts, almost looking like the belts could slip down and off. Actually, if you get the right tightness around your butt, the belt stays in place better than when it's on your hips. While your hips move side-to-side and cause twisting of the belt, your butt tends to keep the race belt in place.

COMPRESSION SOCKS / CALF SLEEVES

Around 2010, *Spot the Triathlete* was a fun game you could play in towns where a race was happening. It was easy to play. You just had to look for the bright pink compression socks pulled up to the person's knees that screamed to the world, "Hey everyone! I'm a triathlete over here, please be super impressed by me!"

At that time, it was almost understood that in order not to be thrashed after a run, you had to train and race in compression socks or compression calf sleeves, and you had to hang out wearing your compression socks after a race or training session. This idea was overblown and, fortunately, good science has meant playing *Spot the Triathlete* is a lot tougher these days.

Compression socks haven't shown any benefit in racing, training or in recovery. Some people claim they feel better after wearing compression socks, but I haven't found a study that even shows a placebo effect.

Racing in compression socks creates a number of problems. First, they take a long time to get on, so you're going to be a slower in transition. Second, feet swell during the race. If you combine a swollen foot with extreme restriction from compression socks, your feet won't function through their natural range of motion.

Compression socks seem to offer a measurable benefit during air travel before or after a race, however. The compression of the sock tends to combat the changing air pressure of flying, so you might feel fresher after travelling.

If you want to wear compression socks in training, or in the name of daily fashion, go for it. I don't recommend them during racing.

RECOVERY BOOTS

Triathletes chilling out in their recovery boots has almost become a meme on Instagram. So many pros and age-group athletes (myself included) can be found wearing them after a hard session. The thought process behind the recovery boots is that the air fills up progressively from your toes to your hips, compressing the blood flow back up into your torso, increasing circulation, reducing inflammation and accelerating recovery.

Everyone claims the boots feel great, and the body feels refreshed after a session. But there haven't been any studies to show this system works. The results of studies are varied, but people keep using the boots. Why?

Personally, I feel the boots do work, but not necessarily in the way you might think. I find they enhance recovery: the time you spend in the boots is forced rest for 45-60 minutes, something triathletes don't do enough of. This alone provides a recovery benefit. Also, the placebo effect is real. If you spend 45-60 minutes in a pair of boots thinking about enhanced blood flow while enjoying what feels almost like a very light, surface-level massage, it may stimulate recovery. In that case, the boots are enhancing recovery, not because of the compression itself.

That said, recovery boots are expensive. If money isn't an object to you, then get a pair. Just don't think they're a crucial part of successful training. Recovery, however, is a crucial part of successful training. You can get a similar effect by standing in a pool or hot tub and chilling out for a bit, focusing more on laying down with your legs elevated each day and getting quality sleep.

HIGH-END RUNNING SUNGLASSES

Sorry to my $220 ROKA GP sunglasses. I love you. You're light. You have great visibility and a huge viewing angle. You stretch nicely to get over my helmet and have the best hinge of any sunnies I've ever used. But for the cash-strapped developing triathlete, who has tens-of-thousands-of-dollars' worth of other purchases they probably want to make, you're not necessary.

Professional triathlete Jesse Thomas, before his first pro win at the 2011 Wildflower Triathlon, bought a ridiculously cheap pair of aviators at a gas station. It wasn't until years later when ROKA ended up developing a lightweight titanium version of those aviators, that Jesse finally stopped using cheap ones in races. If the best in the world aren't using super-duper, high-end shades, it's not an expense you need to stress about.

If you're looking for high-end glasses, though, I love the ROKA shades I mentioned above. It doesn't have to be those shades, though. Look for something with a big viewing angle, ideally something where you can't see much, if any, of the frame. Look for something lightweight so your ears and face don't get tired from having to hold them up (which is something worth worrying about in an event as long as an IRONMAN). Look for polarized lenses to take the glare off the road surface. Look for glasses that are flexible enough to get knocked around in a transition bag and not break.

Pro tips:

- Wind-tunnel testing shows that, on the bike, there's not much benefit to using an integrated helmet with a visor versus using a helmet and sunglasses. Use whatever you like.

- If your glasses get smudged up and you can't seem to get the grease off, use a little bit of dish soap to wash them. Soap breaks down the grease caused by your sweat.

- If you wear prescription glasses, most races will have a glasses station set up immediately coming out of the swim. You can save time in transition by going with a helmet and prescription shades.

INSOLES

A friend of mine, a casual runner, once told me his foot pain was so bad, he had to get custom orthotics made for all of his shoes. He said that once he got the orthotics, he was able to run. I asked him if the podiatrist had prescribed any foot strengthening exercises or had recommended going to see a physiotherapist. He said no. I was nervous for him. I lean towards addressing the imbalance or the lack of strength that led to an injury so the injury goes away, as opposed to managing it and not addressing its root cause.

My buddy began running again. That started a several-year cycle of: get orthotics, feel slightly better, run a little, get injured, get new orthotics, feel slightly better, run a little, get injured, etc. He kept getting bigger, more structured orthotics every time he got injured—while not addressing the injury's cause. This reached a point that walking, standing and running was so painful that he had a hard time keeping fit at all.

A recent study[7] suggested that both orthotics and insoles make running economy worse, meaning that they make running harder.

Of course, I'm not a doctor. But whenever a specialist advises to take a pill, or slap a device onto your body, and doesn't want to address the root cause of the issue you're dealing with, I'd be cautious. In the case of foot pain, I'd recommend an approach using both a podiatrist to make sure the structure of the foot is completely healthy, and a running-specific physiotherapist to make sure your movement patterns are functioning properly.

In general, treat orthotics as a last resort, and try everything you can to rehabilitate the issue first.

SPECIAL NOTE: TRAINING BUDDY

A special shout out needs to go to training partners around the world. While they're not a piece of gear, they're probably the most beneficial addition to your training you can make.

---

[7] https://www.ncbi.nlm.nih.gov/pubmed/31423908

After suffering from overtraining in 2017, I decided to leave the triathlon group I'd been training with to make sure I didn't over-extend myself in any workouts so I could recover and not do any more damage to myself. I knew I'd miss out on the group aspect, but I was excited to see what I was capable of with workouts designed specifically for me, and not a group.

Over the following two years, while I got healthy again, set PRs that I never thought possible, and did the best training of my life, the training became mentally difficult, and by the end of the second year of training alone, my motivation to train was lagging.

I talked to Sarah True about this at the end of the 2019 season. She said she felt some of the same things after a couple years of training by herself in New Hampshire. Her husband, Ben, also found it a bit of a grind after years of doing the same.

Training partners can be both the best thing for your training and the worst. If you're altering the intention of a workout just to fit in with a group, that's not a great thing. For example, if you're supposed to go for a long run with a heart rate cap of 135 beats per minute, but your group turns the weekly long-run into a pissing contest where your heart rate is 155 beats per minute, you're going to dig yourself a hole and cause your workouts for the rest of the week to suffer.

Group workouts can be tough. Someone tends to push a little too hard, taking the whole group into the low return on investment zone of training. That low ROI zone takes a toll on the body, but doesn't do anything to make you faster.

On the other hand, a good training partner who's similarly paced and has like-minded intentions, will make time fly much faster during the long workouts, and make the hard efforts seem easier during the hard workouts.

The key to finding a good training partner (or group) is to find someone with the same understanding of training. Look for someone who understands that an easy run means REALLY easy, and that you aren't going to push into low return on investment training zones. That's perhaps the biggest thing to look for. The intense runs can be done on looped courses, or a track, so you don't need to be constantly running side-by-side.

When you start training with a partner or a group, don't worry about getting your exact workout in the way you want. Be flexible, but keep the same intent you had coming into the session. If you've got a 1:30 long easy run planned, and the group goes for 1:45 hours but stays easy, that's cool. If you want to do four-minute intervals, and your partner wants to do eight-minute intervals, that's cool too. The downside to training with other people happens when you abandon your workout intent, turning a long easy run into a long hard run, or an intense run into a recovery run when that's not what you should be doing that day.

Finally, one time-saving (and marriage-saving) hack my wife, No Triathlon Kim, and I figured out, when I was spending all my free time running in preparation for 2019 Challenge Roth: we could get in some quality time if she rode her bike alongside me during my long runs. It became several hours a week where we could hang out together and chat. It made a huge difference in my enjoyment of the training, particularly for the ultra-long, long runs.

Try your best to find a training partner or group, only slightly altering your training plan to make it work. Soon enough, you'll be thankful you did.

CHAPTER 5

RUNNING OFF INTO THE SUNSET

All the run training in the world can be undone on race day by bad execution. In preparation for 2019 Challenge Roth, I was working through my race plan with Dr. Dan Plews, who said, "Most sports are 90% preparation and 10% execution. Triathlon is more like 50% preparation and 50% execution."

One athlete I was working with in preparation for an IRONMAN did all of his training bang on, made huge gains and was well prepared for his race. He had a time goal in mind for the bike, but due to the hilly nature of the course, he realized he was off his time goal. So, he cranked the final one-hour of the bike extra hard to reach that goal. That caused him to have to walk for a big chunk of the marathon because his legs were toast.

I went into IM 70.3 Campeche (Mexico) in 2017 thinking I was so incredibly well prepared that I had the potential to set huge personal bests. I got off the bike feeling great, so instead of sticking close to my race plan, I ran the first five kilometers off the bike in 20 minutes, way above my target of a 22:30 per five kilometer pace. I went on to suffer through the run, doing the next 5 km sections in an average of 26:33 each, clocking a 1:45 half-marathon, which was 10 minutes off my goal. It was not awful, but enough to ruin my planned race.

Or, there's another athlete I know who did all the training right, but didn't plan out their nutrition until a week before the race. They picked up an all-in-one fluids + calories + electrolytes mix (not something I recommend) and proceeded to cramp their way through the final 20 km of their half-IRONMAN bike and through the entire run, missing their sub-seven hour time goal by over 15 minutes.

You can do a great training build to a race, then on race day, end up undoing all of it with improper nutrition, pacing, gear, transitioning and overall race management. Aside from one bad race where I changed my bike position two days before the race and ended up cramping from head to toe, and some small underperformances from my race goal, I've been consistent with race execution. Throughout 2018 and '19, I generally finished within just a few minutes of my planned/goal times. In some cases, I even exceeded my own expectations.

Running is often the spot where races unravel, but sometimes the issue isn't with the run itself. I'll touch briefly on several key decisions you'll need to make before you hit the run course, such as bike pacing and nutrition. But those are big topics. I'd encourage you to dive into those items in their full detail with our other Foundations series books: *Triathlon Swimming Foundations, Triathlon Bike Foundations* and *Triathlon Nutrition Foundations.*

Now, I'll tell you some of the very easy-to-use strategies for letting the hard work you've done in training show itself on race day. Often, less is more. Be calm, and simplify your race execution with the strategies below.

BIKE PACING

When a race goes wrong for most athletes, it happens in the run. Thus, when this is the case, most athletes will go back to the drawing board to pick apart their run. But it's what happens leading up to the run that's a factor in determining whether you'll be able to execute the run you're capable of.

As I mentioned at the start of this book, when I raced Challenge Roth in 2019, and for the first time ever in a full distance triathlon, my 3:24 marathon run was the strongest of my three disciplines. I later spoke on our podcast with Dr. Dan Plews who coached me to Roth. Dan said the run was obviously my standout performance, but even he didn't know if that was due to my run fitness or my bike fitness.

In order to have a good run, you need to be strong enough on the bike that you're able to complete the bike portion of your race feeling slightly taxed but completely able to execute a good run. To save some trees and keep this section under 300 pages, I'll just say that if you want to work on your bike, go pick up *Triathlon Bike Foundations*. This book lays out a system where age-group triathletes can develop into strong triathlon cyclists with only two key workouts a week.

That said, I will address pacing in this book because it's a relatively easy topic to cover and it applies to you whether you're a super strong biker or you're just starting out. We lay out in *Triathlon Bike Foundations* the ideal rates of perceived exertion for the different triathlon distances:

- ➤ **Sprint**: 8/10
- ➤ **Olympic**: 7/10
- ➤ **Half-IRONMAN (70.3):** 6-7/10
- ➤ **IRONMAN:** 6/10

Of course, you might have been hoping for a power range or a heart rate ceiling to shoot for in a triathlon, but starting with a specific metric is a backward way of trying to dial in your pace because not everyone can hold the exact same power or heart rate numbers.

Instead, figure out your target race heart rate or power number by using the rate of perceived exertion guidelines above in your training. In your main brick workouts that you'll do in the final two months before your race, perform larger and larger amounts of time at the perceived effort levels indicated above, followed by a brick run.

As you do these long brick workouts more often, you'll start to get a feel for what's too hard and what's too easy. If your run feels incredibly easy after the bike, then you can bike a little harder as your race effort. If you're really stiff and have a terrible run, you may have biked too hard and need to back off a bit.

Perform this workout over and over, and you'll eventually find the so-called race pace feel. You'll also be able to look back after your workouts to see what your heart rate or power numbers were when you successfully tapped into your race pace feeling. Use this test repeatedly in your training to further dial in your race pace plan on the bike which will set you up for a good run.

This brick workout guideline is cramming about 140 pages of *Triathlon Bike Foundations* into one page. If you want to dive into being prepared for the bike, go grab that book on Amazon or get the digital download version at triathlonbikefoundations.com.

RACE NUTRITION

Very much like the bike book was crammed into one page in the last section, I'll try to cover the basics of a race nutrition strategy here. Again, if you want to dive into exactly how to nail nutrition for your race, go grab the Triathlon Nutrition Foundations book on Amazon or at mymottiv.com/triathlonnutritionfoundations/.

The starting point I recommend is to calculate how many calories you'll burn (and need to replace) during your race. We've made this easy for you with a calculator that you can download at mymottiv.com/runfoundations, which customizes how many calories you need based on your race distance, your race time and your weight.

That calculator is the key starting point to get your race nutrition right. Guidelines on nutrition packages aren't customized to your weight or your pace, but the calculator will cure the majority of nutritional issues you might have.

Once you've used that calculator to determine how many calories you need to take in during you race, the next step is to create a fueling schedule to provide you with those calories. This is the basic schedule we recommend:

- ➤ 20-30 minutes before race: one serving of calories.
- ➤ Five minutes after start of the bike and once your breathing has settled down: large sip of fluid.

➢ Take fluid in every five minutes at a pace of roughly 16 ounces per hour.

➢ 10 minutes after start of bike: first serving of calories.

➢ Take calories roughly every 20 minutes thereafter but customize this time interval so you reach even intervals and your calorie intake target.

*Increase your caloric intake by about 10% on the bike and decrease the calories you'll intake by about 10% on the run, where it's harder to ingest a lot of calories.

This might be hard to understand without seeing an example, so we'll lay out how you might plan your nutrition for a five-hour 70.3 where you need to intake 1,000 calories:

	TOTAL CALORIES
30 mins before race: 90 calories	**90**

35-minute swim: no calories

2:45-hour bike

• 4:25 hours of racing: 4.5 16-ounce bottles of fluid, each with 20 calories	**180**
• 10 minutes after start of bike: 70 calories	**250**
• Every 20 minutes, 7 more feeds: 7 x 70 calories	**740**

1:40-hour run

• Every 20 minutes, 5 more feeds: 5 x 50 calories	**990**

Why take in food every 20 minutes? Why more calories on the bike than on the run? Should I take solids, liquids or an all-in-one? (I'll answer that now: don't ever take an all-in-one.) These questions require long answers, which is why I recommend getting *Triathlon Nutrition Foundations* (if it's not yet published at the time you're reading this, it's coming very soon), if you want to take your nutrition plan seriously for your race. And I recommend you do, because without the proper fuel, you can't properly operate.

If you decide to just use the calorie intake calculator we've provided here and not grab the nutrition book, that's totally fine. Just keep these points in mind:

- Smaller feedings roughly every 20 minutes is ideal.
- Solids on the bike (chews, bars or real food) and liquids on the run (Coke or gels) is the safest approach and it's what studies say creates the best results.
- If your stomach starts getting upset, keep taking in calories, but switch to water for your fluid.
- For your fluid, use a light electrolyte drink with a small number of carbs in it, something like 20-40 calories per bottle is enough to help with fluid absorption but not so much that it becomes hard to digest.

If you've biked at a good pace, done your nutrition properly and completed the run training we've laid out for you, then it's time to get into transition and show off all the run strength you've built.

RUN SETUP IN TRANSITION 2

One of the most requested videos people ask for on my YouTube channel is on how to have a fast transition. I've done a couple videos on transition, which you can find by YouTube searching "Triathlon Taren Transition". But people still ask for a checklist, specifics and an exact formula for transition.

It's great that athletes are thinking about how they can improve their transition times. It's free speed. If you can be a minute faster in transition, that's almost as good as running three seconds faster per kilometer in a 70.3. Some people take many, many minutes to get in-and-out of transition. If you're shaving off two, three, even four minutes in transition, you're not making the race any harder on yourself. You're essentially making your run faster without extra effort.

Ever since I started racing 70.3s, my transitions have been fast. If you look up my times on Obstri.com, there was a string of three races from March 2017 to June 2018 where my Transition 2 was the fastest in all three races. I can tell you this: there's no one best fast transition setup, but there's an approach you can take for fast transitions.

The approach I use for fast transitions that works every single time, is to do as little as possible while stationary, and as much as I can while I'm in the first few hundred meters of the run.

If you YouTube search "Triathlon Taren Puerto Rico" for the video titled "Half-IRONMAN 70.3 Puerto Rico 2019 Race Day | As Good as a PB", at 2:58 into the video, you'll see 15 seconds of my Transition 2 from that race. This was the third fastest transition for my age group in that race. There are a couple of things I do to give a nice balance of preparation for the run and a speedy transition:

I put on socks in transition. The socks already have a bunch of baby powder in them so they slip on quicker and my feet are dry so they're less likely to blister. In 2018 IM 70.3 Coeur D'Alene, I didn't use socks for the run and had the second fastest T2 in the entire race, but my heel bled badly on the run. I still ran well, but you make a trade-off between comfort and speed in transition.

In Puerto Rico, I also put on a running race belt in transition. Normally, if the swim is a wetsuit swim (this race was not), I'll jam the race bib under the wetsuit before the race starts, trying not to crumple it. This saves time. The race belt is already on, so you don't have to take the few seconds to put it on in transition.

Then the biggest thing you can see for a moment in that video, at 2:04 in Transition 1 and at 3:07 in Transition 2, is that I do things while moving forward. In T1, while most athletes were stopping to get sunscreen put on, I grabbed a spray can of sunscreen from the volunteers and sprayed it on while running through transition. In T2, while most athletes are getting themselves prepped for the run while standing or sitting stationary, I grabbed my running hat (I had pre-stuffed everything I needed for the run inside the hat) and went off. As I moved out of transition, I started pulling things out of the hat, one at the time, during the first few hundred meters of the run: nutrition out of the hat and into the pockets, shades out of the hat and on my face, sunscreen out of the hat and into a hand, hat on my head, spray on sunscreen, run!

Hawaii IRONMAN podium winner Sarah Crowley once told me she rolls the top of her race kit down and stuffs it into her swim skin. Then, in Transition 1, as she's running toward her bike, she gets the swim skin down and is putting the top on and zipping it up. As she put it, "You've got to do something when you're running through transition. It might as well make you faster."

That's the key to a fast transition: do as much preparation as you can before the race starts (or in the first few minutes of the bike and run), so you have very little to do while in the actual transition zones. Here are some examples:

Have all your bike nutrition pre-stored (taped to the bike, in a storage box or in your race kit pockets) prior to the race start

I like using a helmet with a visor. It eliminates having to put on sunglasses in Transition 1, and it's easier to put on shades after Transition 2 while you're on the first few hundred meters of the run, than it is to try to put on shades during the first few hundred meters of the bike

I like using a hat for the run because I can put absolutely everything I need into it, then grab it and head off for the run. I won't forget to do anything in Transition 2 because if an item's in the hat, something needs to happen with it.

Pour baby powder into your shoes and socks (if you're using socks) prior to the race so your feet slip in easily

If you're going sockless for a shorter distance race, smear Vaseline all around the inside of the shoe to reduce the chance you'll get blisters

Use elastic laces on your shoes, or make sure they can be slipped on easily without elastic laces

BONUS: If you're not using elastic laces, pre-tie a double knot in your laces so they don't come undone during the run

If you need to put on sunscreen for the run, do so while you're running. Sunscreen is a non-negotiable for hot weather races, especially if you burn easily. Allowing your skin to burn during the race takes a toll on your body. You won't notice it's happening, but if you burn, you'll naturally slow down.

One final note about transition: while this entire section is about being faster in transition, you don't want to be rushed, especially in the longer distances. After reading this section, you might think you need to bomb through transition as fast as possible, like the elite ITU athletes, whose success in a race depends on getting out as fast as possible. That's not the case for us amateurs.

For Sprint and Olympic races, you want a mindset of controlled quickness. In these races, your heart rate will be elevated because the race is just that fast. Don't hurry through transition so much that you feel scattered and potentially forget something. Be controlled and prepared.

In 70.3 and IRONMAN distance races, heart rate management is important in transition. If you blast through transition and skyrocket your heart rate, you might not ever be able to bring it back down. This will set you up for failure, particularly on the run, before you've even gotten out of T2.

Instead of scrambling through transition, jog in a controlled pace that you'd consider a recovery run pace, around 30-60 seconds per kilometer (or 48 seconds -1:36 minutes per mile), slower than your race pace. Keeping your heart rate nice and low in transition will allow you to keep it that way during the rest of the race. You'll burn fewer calories and be less taxed toward the end of the race where drops in speed are common. If you can avoid those speed decreases, you'll pass a lot of people!

PACING

Choosing a pace is the final, crucial step in making sure you're able to show off your run fitness on race day. We want to get you as close to your absolute fastest possible run, without going too far, risking a bad race.

On the MōTTIV training app, we get asked all the time, "How do I know what my race pace is?" I often respond with, "It's your race pace," which I'm sure might lose us some athletes to coaches willing to say these athletes need to do some kind of running test. From there, their race pace is X percent of what they ran in that test. This isn't how racing works, though.

The problem with these race pace determining tests is that they're performed on one day, in one set of conditions. Those conditions are certainly going to be different than on race day. You'll be tapered on race day, the course terrain might be different, you might be racing in a different climate, you might have gotten a crappy sleep or have some race day nerves. Everything is different on race day. If you have a set-in-stone type of metric you're trying to reach that was forged in completely different conditions, you'll be set up to underperform.

Instead, I want you to develop what a potential race pace *feels like* in your training. Developing this innate sense of what you're capable of means you'll be able to feel your way to your best possible race, no matter the circumstances. Here's how you can start to figure out your race pace:

General rate of perceived exertion guidelines for pacing each race:

> **Sprint**: 8/10
> **Olympic**: 7/10
> **Half-IRONMAN (70.3)**: 6-7/10
> **IRONMAN**: 6/10

After your weekly long bike rides, perform a brick run.

Around two to three months out from your race, perform longer portions in some of these brick runs at what you might think is a race pace.

If you feel stiff, your body cramps up, or you fade significantly towards the end of the brick run, you've either gone too hard in the bike or the run.

Adjust your pace up-and-down until you can find one that feels like you can complete that brick run easily, but is slightly challenging. This'll be close to the pace you can execute in a race.

Use the pace number that you just determined as a guideline on race day, but more importantly, you should also listen to the signals your body is giving you.

If you get close to your target pace and it feels awful, back off and you might be able to build back up to it later. If you build up to your target race pace and it feels incredibly easy, hold that target. If it still feels easy in the final 25% of the race, then pick up the pace.

You've now got your target race pace figured out. The only thing left to do is execute on race day with a solid run pacing strategy. Racing, particularly the longer distances, isn't as simple as going out and running your exact target pace from the start. With the pacing strategy you're about to learn, you'll save your legs from being overcooked and you'll be able to turn the screws on your competitors when you're feeling good.

One of the trends we've seen after interviewing countless professional triathletes on our Triathlon Taren Podcast, and meeting a lot of them in person, is that they break their races up into chunks. They'll have different goals for certain sections of the bike and run, which takes some of the mental load off of their brains. "Go run 10.5 km four times" somehow sounds easier than, "Go run 42.2 km."

Think about when you've had a mentally grueling day at work and you still have a workout to complete before you hit the hay. Getting the motivation to do that workout is hard. Compare that to a more normal day, where everything is under control and you're mentally fresh when you leave work. In that case, it's easy to go do a workout, right? This is because mental fatigue lowers motivation, and even performance.

Studies[8] suggest that mental strain affects everything. In a race, this means you have to take care of your mental state and make sure you don't lose your mental edge, or you'll likely fade toward the end.

Becoming mentally tough becomes imperative the longer you race; a Sprint triathlon is so short that by the time you start getting mentally tired, the race is pretty much over. In an IRONMAN, your mind starts wandering before you're anywhere close to halfway done. Fortunately, with the right training, your mind will naturally toughen up.

In both 2014 and '17 when I started to bump-up my longer training swims in preparation for the two marathon swims I was embarking on, I started completing training swims longer than 90 minutes—and those swims seemed incredibly long. But after a few months of gradually increasing the once-per-week-long swim from 90 minutes to upward of four hours, a half hour seemed to go by quickly. My perception of time seemed to change.

If you YouTube search "Triathlon Taren 37 km swim" and go to 3:57, you'll see my friend, Jacques (one of the two other swimmers I did the swim with), telling our friend, Pat, "Just 10 kilometers left." We had trained our bodies to swim for a long time, but more importantly, our perception of what a long

---

8 https://www.ncbi.nlm.nih.gov/pmc/articles/PMC6107844/

distance was had become so wacky that swimming 10 km seemed like a short distance. If you follow the gradual training build up we recommend in our books and on the MōTTIV training app, changes like this will happen to you too, and no matter what distance race you decide to enter, you will come to view the distance as a cake walk.

All of that said, even if you've done the right training, it still helps to take some of the load off your brain. It'll make executing the race much easier if you mentally break-up the race into smaller chunks, particularly on the run.

I recommend using kilometers to break up your run because a) kilometers will be used as course markers everywhere in the world whereas miles might not be and b) using kilometers creates more sections, making it easier mentally because the sections are shorter. Sorry, my American friends.

Here's how we recommend breaking up the run for each of the various distances. Use your watch to manually calculate your pace at the distance markers on the course, or set your watch for an alert at each kilometer split:

Sprint:

There isn't much of a course strategy to a Sprint because it's so short that by the time you start to get into a good groove, you're probably done. But even with that said, despite what the name of the distance says, this run isn't an outright sprint. Of course, when you watch pro and elite level ITU triathletes, you'll see them running at speeds similar to 5,000 m and 10,000 m track running races. But these athletes aren't us. Age grouper races should be more evenly paced and many levels down from these all-out efforts by the top one percent of the top one percent in our sport.

Use the first kilometer of the run to build up to your target run pace over the first 500 meters, then over the following 500 meters check in with your body to see how your target race pace is feeling. Get a sense of whether it's going to be too hard or too easy.

If the pace feels too hard, back it off a little. If the pace feels too easy, it's best to maintain the pace.

Check-off your pace goals at each one-kilometer mark and focus on running five good kilometers with fast foot turnover and good upright posture.

If by the final kilometer your pace still feels a little too easy, pick up the pace to a fast effort and see how much time you can gain to the finish.

Olympic:

An Olympic distance triathlon is where you'll start to benefit from mentally breaking up the race into chunks. An Olympic distance run is aerobic, meaning it's a paced, controlled run; at no point should you feel like you're close to a max effort level.

Just like in a Sprint race, use the first kilometer of the run to build up to your target run pace over the first 500 meters. Over the following 500 meters, check in with your body to see how your target race pace is feeling. Get a sense of whether it's going to be too hard or too easy.

If the pace feels too hard, back it off a little. If the pace feels too easy, it's best to maintain the pace.

Break up the Olympic distance run into kilometers.

After your pace check in the first kilometer, focus on six kilometers controlled and smooth, executing a good race that feels almost easy.

Once you reach the seven-kilometer mark, check in with your pace and calculate how much you've got in the tank. Either pick up the pace for the final three kilometers or push hard to maintain your effort. You should have paced your first seven kilometers so there's not a significant (if any) drop off in pace in the final three kilometers.

Half-IRONMAN:

A half-IRONMAN race is where it really starts getting crucial to pace yourself properly and break the race up into stages. Even the fastest runners are only doing the 70.3 run in 1:10, which is long enough to be a 100% endurance run. Most of us are running the 70.3 run in 1:45 or more, which is a long run even if you didn't have to swim 1.9 km and bike 90 km beforehand as a warm up.

After finishing my race at IM 70.3 Atlantic City in 2019, I walked backwards down the course all the way to Transition 2 to pick up my bike. The way the course was laid out, I got to see basically the entire run course in reverse, from finish to start. That was the first time I'd ever seen the regression from how people run close to the finish line versus how triathletes look coming out of T2.

At about every point along the run course from the finish line to the start of the run, athletes looked better and better, showing a clear trend that people run out too fast and gradually deteriorate throughout the run. This isn't what we want. We want the pace to be as close to even as possible throughout, with maybe a 10-15 second per kilometer (18-27 seconds per mile) drop in pace from the start of the run to the finish.

I've made this mistake before, and I've paid for it. At IM 70.3 Campeche in 2017, I felt so great running out of transition, I brought my pace down to 4:00 kilometers for the first 5 km (which was WAY over pace.) I was even pumping-up the crowd, getting them to cheer for the athletes along the course. Quickly though, the wheels fell off. Over the rest of the run, I deteriorated so much that my second to last kilometer was a 5:42. I was on the struggle bus for the entire run, and instead of running the target 4:30/km average pace I had wanted, I ran a 5:00/km average pace.

Don't do what I did in Campeche. Set yourself up for success by dosing your effort for the best run possible with this strategy:

➢ Run easy out of Transition 2. No matter how good you feel, hold back in the first two kilometers.

➢ In the first five kilometers, build up to your target pace and no faster. This is going to take effort because you'll feel great around the crowds and your muscles aren't yet smashed up. Athletes who don't know how to dose their effort will also be passing you. Don't worry. You'll move past them soon enough.

➢ From kilometers five to 10, hold your target race pace or even run just slightly (and I mean very slightly) above your target race pace.

➢ At the 10 km mark, check in with your body to see how you feel. If slightly over your target pace feels good, great. Hold that, but don't pick up the pace. If going slightly above your target pace feels hard, back down to your target pace.

➢ If you've dosed your pace correctly, by the 15 km mark, you'll be tired. Don't worry, this is what we want. You'll have to dig deep to push through the fatigue to try to keep your pace as close as possible to your target race pace. Push hard and be tough. Try to run smooth, focusing on good form: upright posture, fast feet and pump those arms!

This variable running pace, where you start easy and then build up to slightly faster than your target race pace, pushing harder at the end, should get your close to your target average race pace while also working with what your body wants to do at every point along the way (and not letting your emotions blow you up).

IRONMAN:

IRONMAN run pacing is important. Pace the IRONMAN run wrong and you'll be one of the giant number of athletes in the sea of carnage walking on the side of the road. Pace the run correctly, you'll blast past tons of people in the final half of the marathon.

In the week before racing my first IRONMAN distance race, I was talking with my coach, Dr. Dan Plews, about how to run the marathon. In addition to being known as one of the best triathlon coaches in the world, Dan also won the 2018 IRONMAN World Championship age group overall title and had the sixth fastest run time of the day overall, including the pro field.

Early in the season, I was doing one-kilometer repeats at 3:30/km (5:38/mile). I had done 19-minute 5 km races years earlier when I wasn't nearly as run fit, meanwhile in tempo running workouts, I could easily hold 4:30/km (7:14/mile) for 60 minutes while still having a nice low heart rate, and I had done 70.3 half-marathons with an average pace of 4:30/km (7:14/mile) when I wasn't nearly as run fit as I'd become in the build-up to this race.

When Dan Plews told me the pace he wanted me to run in the race, I was shocked: 5:00/km (8:03/mile)! As Dan said, "That's probably a lot slower than you were expecting. The goal is to keep you running, not walking. Trust me, if you're still running that pace at the end of the marathon, you'll pass a lot of people."

I was skeptical. But I trusted Dan. Come race day, he was exactly right. Not only did I pass people in the second half of the marathon, but I passed people throughout the entire marathon. Lots of athletes who went out too hard on the bike and during the first few kilometers of the run ended up walking, shuffling and standing on the side of the road. If you can keep a steady pace that allows you to run the entire marathon without stopping, you'll have a race you may never have thought possible. Here's how to do it:

➤ Choose a pace that is quite a bit slower than you think you're capable of, using your heart rate ceiling as a guide. For reference, in the build-up to the Challenge Roth race described above, I had been able to run easily for hours on end under my heart rate ceiling at a 5:05/km pace (8:11/mile) and this pace felt like a walk. My target race pace was just seconds faster per kilometer.

➤ If you're on a hilly course, your target pace will likely be even a little slower than you'd like because your pace might increase by 30 seconds per kilometer on uphills (which take a long time) but your pace might only drop by 15-20 seconds per kilometer on downhills (which don't take much time).

➤ Use kilometer splits to break up the race.

➤ During the first 10 kilometers that slow pace is GOOD, do not have even a single kilometer that's more than three to five seconds faster per kilometer than that pace. This means, if you've paced the bike properly as we prescribed in *Triathlon Bike Foundations*, you'll have to hold yourself back during these first 10 km of the run.

➤ During the second 10 km, if you feel good, allow your pace to be dictated by what feels good. But again, keep your target pace in mind and only allow your kilometer splits to vary from the target pace by five to 10 seconds per kilometer.

➤ Let your pace vary on uphills and downhills by roughly 30 and 15 seconds, respectively. This should keep your effort level similar to the target average pace.

➤ After the 20 km mark, be prepared to dig for your target pace. At some point, around 20-35 kilometers, the race is going to get tough. Really tough. But if you've chosen the right pace, you'll still be able to keep that pace. You'll just have to dig deep to do it.

➤ If you've chosen the right pace and executed the first 20 km properly, you'll have to find motivation to keep that pace up. It's going to hurt, but it is entirely possible. Think about why you're racing, what executing the best race of your life will mean to you, what message not giving in will send, and what you're trying to qualify for. Get mean. Get happy. Whatever it takes to keep you working is what you're going to have to do. This is where you find out what you're really made of in life. It's a feeling like nothing else.

When the marathon gets tough, focus on good form and not letting your body seize up. This is going to take effort, but it's critically important to executing the race you want. Focus on a few key touch points. The ones I like: stay upright, pump the arms and keep your feet fast.

Regardless of the distance, if you've chosen the right pace and executed your race plan well, the feeling of crossing that finish line will be like few other moments you'll experience in your life. You'll feel strong, accomplished and know you gave it everything you had. Don't expect the run to feel easy. But if triathlons were easy, would we even be interested in doing them?

Get across that finish line feeling like you're in more control of the race than the race is in control of you, and you'll be ready to move on to the next race, continuing to make yourself better, faster and stronger!

CHAPTER 6

YOUR NEXT STEPS (see what I did there?)

They say a journey of a thousand miles begins with a single step. I'm never a fan of cliché sayings like that. I think they lose their meaning after we hear them countless times. But in the case of this book, that saying is true.

Too often I hear triathletes say they'll start running after they get the right shoes, or they can't make progress because they don't have a good enough running watch, or that they're not built for running so they don't focus on it, or that they don't run at all because they get injured when they run. This is a shame. Of the three sports we triathletes do, running is the one we're born to do the most.

We didn't evolve to swim. Swimming was something early humans would do only if things went horribly wrong. Yet we somehow thought it was a good idea to take up a sport in an environment we can't actually breathe in. And our ancestors certainly didn't survive by chasing down their meals on a carbon road bike. No, our grandparents ran to school. Our great-great grandparents ran to the nearest town. Our great-great-great x10 grandparents ran every day to chase down their next meal. The human body has evolved to run for a long distance better than almost any animal in the world.

I believe the reason a lot of us don't run isn't because we don't want to run. It's because the way the world is built makes it hard for us to run. We sit in cars, at our desks and on the couch. Our hips are tight. Our nice big glutes, meant for running, don't work very well. We've covered the world with unnaturally hard concrete surfaces, making running around most areas hard on the body. And publications contrive new articles every day, week, or month with so many recommendations about what runners "have to" do, that everyone is confused about how to even start.

Put all these factors together, and it's a recipe for triathletes to throw their hands up in the air and, unfortunately, think they won't ever run well in a triathlon. They envision a lifetime of cramped runs. Races ending in barely getting over the finish line, instead of charging though it feeling like the badass they wanted to be when they originally got into triathlon.

I've experienced every one of these challenges. I could barely run nonstop to the end of the block when I first got into triathlon. I had to break up runs into running the length of one house then walking the length of a house. When I finally did build up my ability to run more, I was constantly injured. I didn't know what good shoes were. I ran in the same $20 sneakers I wore to lift weights in the gym. And, even after several years in triathlon, I suffered through every single one of my runs because I didn't know how to properly train for a race besides just going out and running.

Fortunately, after years of trial and error, I learned what worked (and what didn't) to solve all of the problems I experienced. And, over the past five years, I've been fortunate to get to know and learn from some of the best coaches in the world, like Dr. Dan Plews, Matt Dixon and Paul Mackinnon. I've also run alongside naturally gifted runners like Sarah and Ben True, and talk to great runners, like Lucy Charles-Barclay and Cameron Wurf, both of whom say running initially didn't come naturally to them. All along the way, I've learned from these great people and incorporated their knowledge into the system you just read about.

Since those days when I struggled to run to the end of my street, I've developed my run into being in the top three percent of some international half-IRONMAN distance races, and in the top six percent of the first IRONMAN distance race I competed in. I'm still not a natural runner. I always have to motivate myself to get out the door for run workouts (and don't even get me started on the lack of motivation to go on the treadmill). I still occasionally get running injuries. My joints tend to get sore. But even with all those challenges, my run has improved significantly, and yours will too with the right approach.

So, what are the next steps for you to get started? Here's the order-of-action items I'd recommend for how to get going on the right foot (pun intended!):

> ➤ If you don't have them already, get some proper running shoes to avoid injury.

> ➤ Use the heart rate zone calculator guide at mymottiv.com/runfoundations to figure out your heart rate cap.

> ➤ Use the training season calculator at mymottiv.com/runfoundations to see the distance you should be running on your long runs.

> ➤ Perform one intense run and one long run each week.

> ➤ Perform the long run as long as the guidelines in the calculators prescribe with most (or all) of the run being under your heart rate cap.

> ➤ Perform intervals in the intense run *INTENSELY*; make sure to make them challenging.

> ➤ If your race is coming up soon, start doing a weekly brick run.

> ➤ Print out the guidelines for terrain, pace, and elevation that you can find at mymottiv.com/runfoundations.

> ➤ GO RUN!

That's it! It's as simple as that. Forget about the fanciest of fancy running shoes, super-expensive clothes, hydration packs, sports nutrition and all the other things you could buy. Forget about the thousands of running articles you've read that all end up giving conflicting advice. With the two-run-per-week system in this book, you'll easily be one of the most prepared triathletes at the start line. Not because you've run yourself into the ground with more miles than everyone else, but because you've focused on the right things to do in the miles you run.

Running is intimidating. It's long and sometimes boring. It can hurt. It's the part of the race where things can unravel the most. But running can also be natural, easy, calming, and provide some great quality time with friends from a running group, or while your partner or a supportive friend cycles alongside you.

What's more, if you put in the miles with the right structure like we've laid out for you in this book, you could easily and predictably turn the run into your strength. Picture yourself getting onto the run in a race and feeling so good, you've got to hold yourself back instead of fight through cramps. Picture yourself running past person after person as you execute your race exactly as you had hoped. And picture yourself getting across the finish line feeling strong, confident and like the athletic badass you always wanted to be, because you raced as well as you could have hoped, thanks to doing right training and giving it your all.

Go run, run enough to make progress, run with good technique, run and have fun, and have a great race!

WHAT'S NEXT

Now that you're done with this book, here are some next steps for you.

1. JOIN THE MōTTIV COMMUNITY

There are so many ways to join the MōTTIV community! Here's how:

Visit us online at mymottiv.com for free resources, valuable training info, and more.

Visit app.mymottiv.com to get signed up to the most accessible triathlon training platform in the world. For a fraction of the price of a one-on-one coach, get a fully customizable, year-round training plan to get you totally prepared for your races, no matter your level of experience!

2. FOLLOW US ON SOCIAL MEDIA

For tips, tricks, training updates and more, follow us on our most active social media channels:

YOUTUBE: youtube.com/triathlontaren

INSTAGRAM: @triathlontaren and @mymottiv

FACEBOOK: facebook.com/triathlontaren

3. SUBSCRIBE TO THE PODCAST

The top-rated triathlon podcast in the world on iTunes, the Triathlon Taren Podcast brings you interviews with the who's-who in triathlon including professional triathletes, inspiring age-groupers and more! Download the podcast wherever you get your favorite podcasts.

4. SHARE THIS BOOK

Please write us a review on Amazon or Goodreads and let your fellow triathletes know about us! Spreading the word helps to reach new readers, to grow the MōTTIV community, and it allows us to bring you more great resources.

THANK YOU! And we'll see ya soon!

ACKNOWLEDGMENTS

To Dr. Dan Plews: Whatever you did getting me to Challenge Roth where the run was actually my standout performance, keep doing it, man. Thanks for your unwavering guidance and your cheeky accent.

To Paul Mackinnon (The Balanced Runner): Your tips on arm swing are gold. And my wife still likes your moustache.

To my pal "Super Dave" Lipchen: One of the best training partners in the business, thanks for letting me drop into your club workouts and allowing me to get my ass kicked by your talented kids.

To Chris McDougall, author of *Born to Run*: You don't know me and I don't run barefoot, but your book got me thinking differently about running and life in general.

To my wife, NTK: Thanks for giving up your Saturday and Sunday mornings through the entire spring of 2019 to ride alongside me during my long runs in preparation for Challenge Roth. Your taste in running music is impeccable.

ABOUT THE AUTHOR

Taren Gesell is a successful age-group endurance athlete who originally became known for his wildly popular YouTube channel, Instagram account and podcast, where he shares tips, tricks, hacks, scientifically backed research, and time-tested knowledge to help new and developing endurance athletes get to their start lines confident and their finish lines strong.

Taren is the founder of MōTTIV, which offers a full-service endurance training app that guides athletes of every ability level. The app offers an inclusive, welcoming community of amateur endurance athletes around the world who are working hard to be the best version of themselves every day!

Find more books by TAREN GESELL on Amazon.com

Triathlon Swimming Foundations

Triathlon Bike Foundations

Triathlon Nutrition Foundations

And instant PDF Downloads available at MyMottiv.com

Visit Today!